Excel

Basic Skills

English and Mathematics

Year 3

Ages 8-9

Get the Results You Want!

PASCAL
PRESS

Contents

Introduction

The **Excel** Basic Skills Workbook series aims to build and reinforce basic skills in reading, comprehension and mathematics.

The series has eight English and Mathematics core books, one for each of the school years Kindergarten/Foundation to Year 7. These are supported by teaching books, which can be used if the student needs help in a particular area of study.

The structure of this book

This book has 30 carefully sequenced double-page units. Each unit has work on Number and Algebra, Measurement and Geometry, and Statistics and Probability in Maths, and Reading and Comprehension, Spelling and Vocabulary, and Grammar and Punctuation in English.

The student's competence in each of the 30 units can be recorded on the marking grid on pages 5 and 7. There are four end-of-term reviews. These are referred to as Tests 1 to 4. They assess the student's understanding of work covered during each term.

How to use this book

It is recommended that students complete each unit in the sequence provided because the knowledge and understanding developed in each unit is consolidated and practised in subsequent units. The workbook can be used to cover core classroom work. It can also be used to provide homework and consolidation activities.

All units are written so that particular questions deal with the same areas of learning in each unit. For example, question 1 in Mathematics is always on Number (addition) and question 11 is always on Measurement (length), and so on. Similarly in the English units question 1 is always on Reading and Comprehension, and question 14 is always on Punctuation. Question formatting is repeated throughout the workbook to support familiarity so that students can more readily deal with the Mathematics and English content.

The marking grids (see the examples on pages 4 and 6) are easy-to-use tools for recording students' progress. If you find that certain questions are repeatedly causing difficulties and errors, then there is a specific **Excel** Basic/Advanced Skills Workbook to help students fully revise that topic.

These are the teaching books of the series; they will take students through the topic step by step. The use of illustrations and diagrams, practice questions, and a straightforward and simple approach will make some of the most common problem areas of English and Mathematics easy to understand and master.

Sample Maths Marking Grid

If a student is consistently getting more than **one in five** questions wrong in any area, refer to the highlighted *Excel* Basic/Advanced Skills title. When marking answers on the grid, simply mark incorrect answers with 'X' in the appropriate box. This will result in a graphical representation of areas needing further work. An example has been done below for the first seven units. If a question has several parts, it should be counted as wrong if one or more mistakes are made.

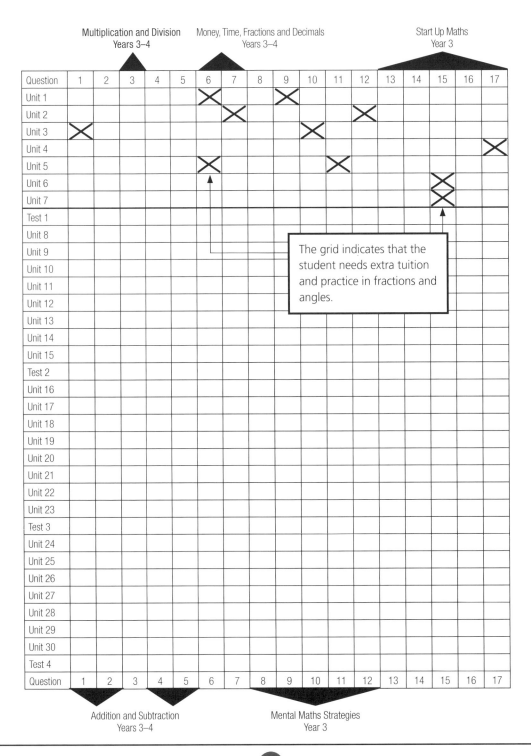

Question	1	2	3	4	5	6	7	8	9	10	11	12	13	14	15	16	17
Unit 1						X			X								
Unit 2							X					X					
Unit 3	X									X							
Unit 4																	X
Unit 5						X						X					
Unit 6															X		
Unit 7															X		
Test 1																	
Unit 8																	
Unit 9																	
Unit 10																	
Unit 11																	
Unit 12																	
Unit 13																	
Unit 14																	
Unit 15																	
Test 2																	
Unit 16																	
Unit 17																	
Unit 18																	
Unit 19																	
Unit 20																	
Unit 21																	
Unit 22																	
Unit 23																	
Test 3																	
Unit 24																	
Unit 25																	
Unit 26																	
Unit 27																	
Unit 28																	
Unit 29																	
Unit 30																	
Test 4																	
Question	1	2	3	4	5	6	7	8	9	10	11	12	13	14	15	16	17

Multiplication and Division Years 3–4

Money, Time, Fractions and Decimals Years 3–4

Start Up Maths Year 3

The grid indicates that the student needs extra tuition and practice in fractions and angles.

Addition and Subtraction Years 3–4

Mental Maths Strategies Year 3

Maths Marking Grid

Question	Addition	Subtraction	Division/Multiplication	Place value	Number patterns	Fractions	Money	Time	Mass	Length	Area	Volume/Capacity	2D shapes	3D shapes	Angles	Symmetry and Transformation	Statistics and Probability
Question	1	2	3	4	5	6	7	8	9	10	11	12	13	14	15	16	17
Unit 1																	
Unit 2																	
Unit 3																	
Unit 4																	
Unit 5																	
Unit 6																	
Unit 7																	
Test 1																	
Unit 8																	
Unit 9																	
Unit 10																	
Unit 11																	
Unit 12																	
Unit 13																	
Unit 14																	
Unit 15																	
Test 2																	
Unit 16																	
Unit 17																	
Unit 18																	
Unit 19																	
Unit 20																	
Unit 21																	
Unit 22																	
Unit 23																	
Test 3																	
Unit 24																	
Unit 25																	
Unit 26																	
Unit 27																	
Unit 28																	
Unit 29																	
Unit 30																	
Test 4																	
Question	1	2	3	4	5	6	7	8	9	10	11	12	13	14	15	16	17

Sample English Marking Grid

If a student is consistently getting more than **one in five** questions wrong in any area, refer to the highlighted ***Excel*** Basic/Advanced **Skills** title. When marking answers on the grid, simply mark incorrect answers with 'X' in the appropriate box. This will result in a graphical representation of areas needing further work. An example has been done below for the first seven units.

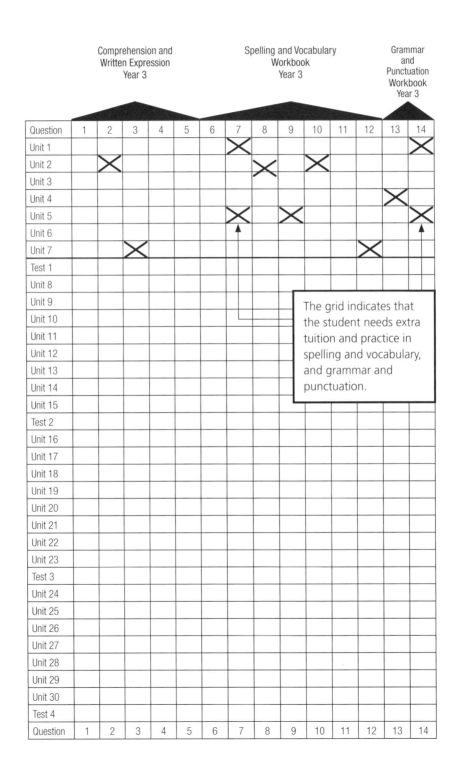

The grid indicates that the student needs extra tuition and practice in spelling and vocabulary, and grammar and punctuation.

English Marking Grid

Question	Reading and Comprehension					Spelling and Vocabulary							Grammar and Punctuation	
	1	2	3	4	5	6	7	8	9	10	11	12	13	14
Unit 1														
Unit 2														
Unit 3														
Unit 4														
Unit 5														
Unit 6														
Unit 7														
Test 1														
Unit 8														
Unit 9														
Unit 10														
Unit 11														
Unit 12														
Unit 13														
Unit 14														
Unit 15														
Test 2														
Unit 16														
Unit 17														
Unit 18														
Unit 19														
Unit 20														
Unit 21														
Unit 22														
Unit 23														
Test 3														
Unit 24														
Unit 25														
Unit 26														
Unit 27														
Unit 28														
Unit 29														
Unit 30														
Test 4														
Question	1	2	3	4	5	6	7	8	9	10	11	12	13	14

Number and Algebra

1.

+	3	5	6	7	9	10
5	8	10	11	12	14	15

2.

−	8	10	9	15	17	26
6	2	4	3	9	11	20

3.

÷	5	3	8	6	9	12
1	5	3	8	6	9	12

4. Write the numeral for sixty-nine ones.  69

5. 10, 20, 30, 40, 50 , 60 , 70 , 80 , 90

6. Write whether this shape is cut into halves or quarters.

   quarters

7. What is the total change from $1 if I buy an ice-cream worth 80 cents? 20¢

Measurement and Geometry

8. Write six seventeen in digital time. 6 : 17

9. Tick the items you estimate to have a mass less than a kilogram.
   (a) a large dog   ☑ a sausage
   ☑ an apple   (d) a television
   ☑ this book   ☑ a ruler

10. Write the short form for two metres. 6 ft

11. How many triangles can you find in this shape?

   12

12. If 4 cups make one litre, then how many cups are needed to make two litres? 8

13. Colour in the hexagon.

14. Name this 3D shape.

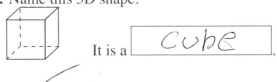   It is a cube .

15. Which angle is smaller (or sharper) than angle (c)? a

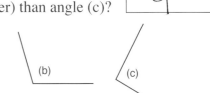

16. Draw in the lines of symmetry on these objects.
   (a)   (b)

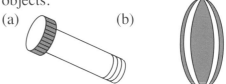

Statistics and Probability

17.

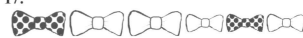

   (a) How many bows are big? 3

   (b) How many bows have spots on them? 2

Quiet pony for sale

When Hannah came with her parents to live in the small town of Bakers Flat, she had to catch the bus to school each day. On the first morning, while she was waiting for the bus to arrive, she saw a notice nailed to a gate on the other side of the highway. "Quiet pony for sale", it read.

Hannah loved horses. That afternoon, she went to the gate and looked over. There in the paddock was the pony. His rough coat was matted with mud, his mane and tail were long and scraggy. He stared at her with sad brown eyes.

"Here, pony!" said Hannah. She felt annoyed that she had nothing to give. The pony stood still.

"I'll bring you something tomorrow," said Hannah, and she hurried home.

Next morning, she took two apples for her lunchbox. Back from school she went straight to the gate. The pony was busy cropping grass.

"Hey, pony!" called Hannah, holding out an apple.

"Come on! Look what I've got for you."

Suddenly, it started to rain.

"Drat!" said Hannah. She threw the apple as far as she could into the paddock.

Next morning, the pony was at the gate.

From Quiet Pony for Sale by Mary Small

Reading and Comprehension

1. Hannah observed the sign while
   (a) the pony was for sale.
   (b) she was waiting for the bus.
   (c) her parents were packing.
   (d) playing in the mud.

2. Another word for *matted* is
   (a) matless.   (b) matey.
   (c) Matilda.   **(d) covered.**

3. The first words Hannah said to the pony were
   (a) "Quiet pony for sale".
   (b) "I'll bring you something tomorrow."
   (c) "Here pony."
   (d) "Come on. Look what I've got for you."

4. The word nearest in meaning to *cropping* is
   (a) planting.
   (b) coiling.
   (c) swallowing.
   (d) cutting.

5. Number these sentences in order (1–4).
   (a) He stared at her with sad eyes. **1**
   (b) Suddenly it started to rain. **4**
   (c) Hannah loved horses. **2**
   (d) She held out an apple. **3**

Spelling and Vocabulary

Rewrite the misspelt words.

6. I always have toast for brekfast.
   breakfast

7. It missed your head by a centimeter.
   _____

Circle the word that has the nearest meaning to the underlined word.

8. Mike ran <u>fast</u> towards the house.
   (a) quickly   (b) far
   (c) recklessly   (d) away

9. Dad <u>repaired</u> the car.
   (a) drove   (b) started
   (c) fixed   (d) examined

Circle the correct word in brackets.

10. I saw him (their, **there**).

11. We didn't see a (sole, **soul**).

12. He (wood, **would**) not do his work.

Grammar and Punctuation

13. Underline the **verbs** in these sentences.

    Go away. Your dog <u>jumps</u> up. His muddy paws soil my clothes.

14. Punctuate and capitalise this sentence.

    the town of broken hill is in new south wales
    The town of broken hill is in New South Wales

Mathematics

Number and Algebra

1.
+	3	0	8	5	10	16
3	6	3	11	8	13	19

2.
−	4	10	12	6	9	13
2	2	8	10	4	7	11

3.
÷	4	8	14	2	6	12
2	2	4	7	1	3	6

4. Write the numeral for one hundred and two. `102`

5. (a) 15, 20, 25, 30, `35`, `40`, `45`

(b) 95, 90, 85, 80, `75`, `70`, `65`

6. Which part of each shape is coloured?
(a) `2 out of 4`
(b) `1 out of 4`

7. Use the least amount of coins to show 55 cents. Draw them in this box.

Measurement and Geometry

8. On each face show the time given.
(a) 3 o'clock   (b) 11 o'clock

9. Which items have been measured in kilograms?
(a) 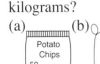 (b) (c) (d)

10. Measure the length of each line.

(a) _____

(b) _____

(c) ____

11. Estimate how many 5 cent coins could fill this shape. Check your estimate.

Estimate [ ]   Check [ ]

12. Write the half-litre water level on this jug.

13. Give the names of the two shapes needed to make this picture.

14. Circle the objects that will roll.

15. Cross out the shape that has no angles.

16. Draw in the shape's reflected half.

Statistics and Probability

17. Rocks | | | | | | | | | |
Shells | | | | |

How many more rocks are there? [ ]

Pandas

Pandas mainly eat bamboo. They will eat meat if they can get it, and they like honey. They also eat grasses, vines and roots, and may even eat flowers, but their diet is mainly bamboo.

Pandas eat twenty-one different kinds of bamboo. They spend up to sixteen hours a day eating. One panda can eat 4500 kilograms of bamboo in a year. That's about four times its height and forty times its body weight.

The panda's head is well designed for its diet. The jaws are very strong and can cut through a tough bamboo stalk. The teeth are thick and wide to crush the bamboo and grind it down.

The panda's 'thumb' helps it to grab the bamboo and hold it steady while it eats. The panda strips away the tough outer layer and eats the soft part inside.

The bamboo stays green even when there are metres of snow on the ground. Pandas keep eating right through the winter. Unlike bears they do not hibernate.

From *Pandas* by Christine Deacon

Reading and Comprehension

1. The panda's diet mainly consists of
    (a) honey.
    (b) meat.
    (c) bamboo.
    (d) vines.

2. Which section of the panda's body is very strong at cutting?
    (a) head   (b) thumbs
    (c) jaw   (d) teeth

3. About how much bamboo can a panda eat in a year?
    (a) 4500 g   (b) 4.5 kg
    (c) 450 kg   (d) 4500 kg

4. Explain why the pandas can keep eating right through the cooler months.

    _____

    _____

5. Number these sentences in order (1–4).
    (a) The teeth are thick and wide.
    (b) Pandas do not hibernate.
    (c) Their diet is mainly bamboo.
    (d) Pandas strip away the tough layer.

Spelling and Vocabulary

Rewrite the misspelt words.

6. I've never tried to halm any of my pets.

    _____

7. My teacher put a bandage on my scrach.

    _____

Circle the word that has the nearest meaning to the underlined word.

8. I'll have it finished by <u>noon</u>.
    (a) morning   (b) 3 o'clock
    (c) midnight   (d) lunchtime

9. The <u>lady</u> owned a Dalmatian.
    (a) mother
    (b) woman
    (c) nurse
    (d) aunty

Circle the correct word in brackets.

10. She (one, won) the race by ten metres.

11. The hungry rats (ate, eight) the tiny crumbs.

12. Have you seen (one, won) of my thongs?

Grammar and Punctuation

13. Underline the **nouns** in these sentences.

    My father is funny. Dad has golden hair and he has no front teeth. His eyes are brown.

14. Punctuate and capitalise this sentence.

    for lunch i had a piece of fish and some chips with tomato sauce

    _____

    _____

    _____

Number and Algebra

1.

+	10	6	9	0	5	16
8						

2.

–	9	7	10	14	8	28
7						

3.

×	5	8	3	7	4	12
2						

4. Write the numeral for four hundred and forty-four.

5. (a) 21, 31, 41, ☐, ☐, ☐, ☐

    (b) 99, 98, 97, ☐, ☐, ☐, ☐

6. Colour one half of each group.

(a)    (b)

7. What is the total change from $2 if I buy an eraser worth $1.70?

Measurement and Geometry

8. Use lines to join the same times together.

    2:30   eight thirty

    10:30   half past ten

    8:30   30 minutes past 2

9. Write the following mass measurements the short way.

(a) ninety-five kilograms

(b) one hundred and two kilograms

(c) twenty-two kilograms

10. The length of your broom is about ☐. Check your answer by using a measuring tape.

11. How many squares make this shape? ☐

12. Find out how many medicine glasses it would take to fill a litre.

Estimate ☐   Check ☐

13. Count the number of △ and ○ in this picture.

△ = ☐

○ = ☐

14. Match the solid shape to its name.

cylinder, cube, sphere, cone, rectangular prism

15. Name this angle.

r _ _ _ _ _   a _ _ _ _ _

16. Cross out the objects that are not divided into halves.

Statistics and Probability

17. 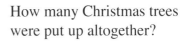 = 3 Christmas trees

How many Christmas trees were put up altogether? ☐

Monday 10th April

Dear Diary,

I'm writing in the taxi on the way to the TV studio. It's 6:45 in the morning and it's just getting light. It was dark and cold when my alarm went off, and I wanted to stay in bed a bit longer. Mum said, "No".

Mr Davies is driving me this morning. He doesn't talk much which is good. I can write more. I can see the grass on the side of the road. It's still wet. It's supposed to be sunny later on. Let's hope so. I hate it when filming stops because of the rain.

My 'call' is for 7:30. Before we finish work each day we are all given a call sheet. It has all the information about what we'll be doing the next day, which scenes we'll be filming (or 'shooting' as they say), and what time everyone has to be at work. Under my name is 'Call time 7:30 am', and 'Scenes 4, 5 and 7'.

Hey, we're here already. I'll run out of the taxi as fast as I can and into the studio so I can stay warm.

From *My Diary* by Jenny Jarman-Walker

Reading and Comprehension

1. The grass on the side of the road is wet from
   (a) rain.
   (b) snow.
   (c) dew.
   (d) water added for the film.

2. What information is not on a call sheet?
   (a) which scenes are to be shot
   (b) the times people are required
   (c) people's names
   (d) the times they leave the studio

3. Mr Davies is
   (a) the author's name.
   (b) the author's father.
   (c) a friend of the author.
   (d) the taxi driver.

4. What will halt filming?

   _____

5. Number these sentences in order (1–4).
   (a) The sun is rising.
   (b) The alarm went off.
   (c) Mum made me get up.
   (d) The taxi arrived.

Spelling and Vocabulary

Rewrite the misspelt words.

6. It made my gums blead. _____

7. I had to poor the cordial into a glass.

   _____

Circle the word that has the nearest meaning to the underlined word.

8. The <u>body</u> of the story is the best part.
   (a) beginning   (b) ending
   (c) middle   (d) stomach

9. That card <u>matched</u> with this one.
   (a) linked
   (b) cut
   (c) made
   (d) marked

Circle the correct word in brackets.

10. My uncle wanted to (buy, by) a motorbike.

11. This train set is not for (sale, sail).

12. (By, Buy) the time you read this, I'll be gone.

Grammar and Punctuation

13. Underline the **pronouns** in these sentences.

    My nanna is famous. She was a well-known poet. Here is a picture of her.

14. Punctuate and capitalise this sentence.

    the thief ran out of peters pizzeria and straight into a bin

    _____

    _____

Number and Algebra

1.

+	7	0	5	10	1	15
10						

2.

–	10	9	15	19	17	29
9						

3.

×	10	15	20	2	0	30
1						

4. Write the numeral for three hundred and twelve.

5. (a) 91, 81, 71, 61, ___ , ___ , ___

(b) 102, 202, 302, ___ , ___ , ___

6. Colour one half of each shape.

(a)   (b)

7. Complete the following:

(a) $1.61 = ___ dollar and ___ cents

(b) $1.97 = ___ dollar and ___ cents

(c) $0.58 = ___ dollars and ___ cents

Measurement and Geometry

8. Complete the labels:

(a)   (b)

___ past   ___ past

9. Arrange the following masses in order from lightest to heaviest.
500 kg, 50 kg, 550 kg, 505 kg, 5 kg

10. Circle the best measure.

(a) 4 L   (b) 8 kg

(c) 5 m   (d) 43 m

(e) 10 cm

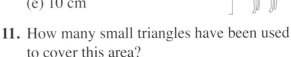

11. How many small triangles have been used to cover this area?

12. How many blocks have been used to make this model?

13. Use a ruler to measure the sides of this rectangle.

(a) How long is it?

(b) How wide is it?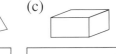

14. Give the name of:

(a)   (b)   (c)

15. Draw 3 angles in order of size. Put the smallest angle on the left and the largest angle on the right.

16. How many axes of symmetry does this shape have?

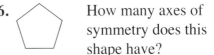

Statistics and Probability

17. Count how many boys there are in 3C.

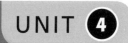

Charlie's damper

A mate of mine, old Charlie, was a bullock driver. In the early days of white settlement there weren't any trucks or trains, so all the heavy hauling had to be done by bullock drays.

While he was on the track, Charlie did all his own cooking. His specialty was damper.

The ingredients for Charlie's damper were plain flour, water, a pinch of salt and some baking powder. He would mix them together with his hands until he had a firm dough. He would shape the dough into a flat cake and place it in a large, well-greased metal pot.

Charlie would put the lid on and bury the pot in the ashes of his fire. Then he would put some hot ashes on top of the lid and, finally, cover the whole lot with hot coals.

It takes about thirty minutes to cook a real good damper. Charlie would push a big piece of twig into it to see if it was ready. If the twig came out sticky, the damper needed to cook a bit longer.

When at last he scooped away the ashes and lifted it out, you could smell that freshly baked, home-made bread for miles.

From *Charlie's Damper* by RL Muddyman

Reading and Comprehension

1. In the early days of white settlement, heavy hauling was done by
    (a) trains.
    (b) bullock drays.
    (c) trucks.
    (d) automobiles.

2. Which ingredient is not included in Charlie's damper?
    (a) yeast   (b) salt
    (c) water   (d) flour

3. The main reason Charlie used a twig was because
    (a) he didn't have a knife to cut it.
    (b) hot ashes landed on the lid.
    (c) the timber mills gave it to him.
    (d) it tested if the damper was ready or not.

4. How long did it take to cook the damper?

    _____

5. Number these sentences in order (1–4).
    (a) His specialty was damper.
    (b) The pot was buried in the ashes.
    (c) Four main ingredients were used.
    (d) Charlie was a bullock driver.

Spelling and Vocabulary

Rewrite the misspelt words.

6. I saw the baloon float away. _____

7. Be careful not to fall off the wramp!

    _____

Circle the word that has the nearest meaning to the underlined word.

8. My <u>mate</u> John is good at knitting.
    (a) neighbour   (b) friend
    (c) cousin   (d) dog

9. The sky was very <u>dark</u>.
    (a) distant
    (b) lonely
    (c) dim
    (d) bright

Circle the correct word in brackets.

10. She was (aloud, allowed) to go to the dance.

11. That dog might (bite, bight) you.

12. My skirt was a light (blew, blue) colour.

Grammar and Punctuation

13. Underline the **nouns** in these sentences.

    Susan plays the piano. She practises every Monday. Her mum plays the guitar.

14. Punctuate and capitalise this sentence.

    the capital of queensland is brisbane

    _____

    _____

Number and Algebra

1.

+	10	20	30	40	50	70
7						

2.

–	10	20	30	40	50	70
7						

3.

÷	10	20	30	40	50	60
5						

4. Write the numeral for:

5. Complete this number pattern.

65, 55, 45, ☐ , ☐ , ☐

6. What fraction of this group is not coloured?

7.   How much is there altogether?

Measurement and Geometry

8. (a) What day is it today?

(b) What date is it today?

(c) What day was it yesterday?

9. Circle the best answer for each of the following.
(a) a bag of sugar—50 kg, 2 kg, 100 kg
(b) a one-day-old baby—3 kg, 30 kg, 13 kg
(c) an adult's mass—12 kg, 75 kg, 200 kg

10. Draw:
(a) a broken line
(b) a zigzag line
(c) a curvy line

11.

(a) How many squares are there? ☐

(b) How many squares contain dots? ☐

12. Name three kitchen-related containers that can hold one litre.

1. _____ 2. _____

3. _____

13. Give the name of each shape.
(a)   (b)   (c)

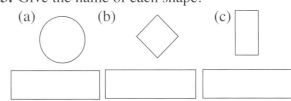

14. Which objects have only flat faces? ✓ or ✗

15. Circle the right angles.

16. Flip this shape to the right.

Statistics and Probability

17.

(a) How many boxes have crosses on them?

(b) Are there more boxes with dots or ticks?

Billy made a blue

It was just after midnight ...

Billy stepped out of bed and put on his navy blue slippers. He crept down the hallway and tried to find his way to the kitchen.

Brrr ... it sure was cold and dark! He clung on to his sky-blue teddy bear and tried to find his way to the kitchen tiles. His woollen socks felt fine on the thick carpet. Keep going Billy, he muttered to himself ... you're nearly there!

After three small steps he found what he was looking for. He grabbed the cookie jar. It's always hidden behind the breadbox.

I love these chocolate chip cookies, he thought to himself. He dipped his fingers into the jar and pulled out his first delicious treat. Mmm ... yum

"Caught you red-handed!" said Mum as she flicked on the kitchen light. "I knew you were the one stealing my cookies. What are you doing out of bed?"

"Oops," said Billy, "but these cookies are so fine and I can't get them out of my mind." He took his first bite and yelled out, "Yuk!" He glanced down and read the label on the jar: SARDINE CRACKERS. He had grabbed the wrong jar!

Reading and Comprehension

1. What was Billy searching for?
   (a) the breadbox
   (b) his teddy bear
   (c) some crackers
   (d) the cookie jar

2. The colour of his teddy bear was
   (a) dark blue.
   (b) red.
   (c) light blue.
   (d) sardine coloured.

3. Billy felt a bit hungry at about
   (a) lunch time.
   (b) noon.
   (c) just after midnight.
   (d) 3 o'clock in the morning.

4. How many chocolate cookies did Billy end up eating? _____

5. Number these sentences in order (1–4).
   (a) Billy put on his slippers.
   (b) Billy read the label.
   (c) He grabbed the cookie jar.
   (d) His mum caught him in the act.

Spelling and Vocabulary

Rewrite the misspelt words.

6. I bought my painting home. _____

7. Put it on the top shelf of the cuboard.

   _____

Circle the word that has the nearest meaning to the underlined word.

8. Close the door behind you.
   (a) tap
   (b) open
   (c) shut
   (d) slam

9. My teacher smiled at me.
   (a) yelled
   (b) grinned
   (c) dove
   (d) sang

Circle the correct word in brackets.

10. The rope was (tide, tied) to the tree trunk.

11. I like the petals on this (flour, flower).

12. Have you (been, bean) to Cairns before?

Grammar and Punctuation

13. Underline the **pronouns** in these sentences.

    They were late. She made an excuse. He didn't accept it. We were angry.

14. Punctuate and capitalise this sentence.

    i bought some roses and carnations for mrs molly

    _____

    _____

Number and Algebra

1.

+	9	10	0	8	5	12
9						

2.

–	10	15	19	17	11	20
10						

3.

×	3	2	4	7	1	10
10						

4. Write the numeral for:

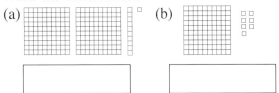

(a) _____

(b) _____

5. Write the next four numbers.

22, 20, 18, ____ , ____ , ____ , ____

6. Shade part of each group to match the fraction given.

(a) one out of eight   (b) 4 out of 20

7. Find the total value of:

(a) two 20c and one 50c coin [ ]

(b) four 5c coins [ ]

(c) one $1 and three 20c coins [ ]

Measurement and Geometry

8. Write these dates the short way.

(a) 4 January 1986 [ ]

(b) 26 June 1998 [ ]

9. Circle the heavier object.
(a) a balloon or a softball?
(b) this book or an exercise book?
(c) a chair or a lunchbox?

10. Is each more or less than a metre?

(a) the height of a door [ ]

(b) your teacher's height [ ]

(c) the length of your hand [ ]

11. How many squares are needed to fill this area? [ ]

12. From one litre of water, we can fill how many:

(a) cups ? [ ]   (b) bowls ? [ ]

13. (a) How many corners has a triangle? [ ]

(b) How many sides has a triangle? [ ]

(c) How many sides has a pentagon? [ ]

(d) How many corners has a pentagon? [ ]

14. (a) Name this shape. [ ]

(b) Draw what you would see if you looked at it from the top. [ ]

(c) Draw what you would see from the front. [ ]

15. Draw a plane shape that has four angles. [ ]

16. Complete this picture if the line drawn is a line of symmetry.

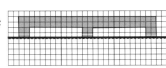

Statistics and Probability

17. (a) Which group has the most items? [ ]

(b) Count the total number of signs. [ ]

Is it the flu?

I didn't feel well on the weekend. On Monday morning I had a pounding headache, so I was sent to the Health Room. My teacher told me to rest on the couch. I still went to school the next day. My eyes were bloodshot and I felt really thirsty.

Wednesday came before I knew it. I still wasn't one hundred per cent, but I forced Mum to let me go to school because it was our Sports Day. I was not going to miss out on the one hundred metre sprint. I knew I could beat Matthew Kolt, but I didn't! I felt awfully hot that day.

On Thursday I noticed a couple more red freckles on my neck. There were some red spots on my face as well. Dad wouldn't let me leave the house. I stayed in bed all day on Friday.

By the weekend there were thousands of red spots all over my body. I tried to count them but lost interest after number twenty. Instead I played dot-to-dot with my black felt pen, but Dad was not impressed!

The doctor said I had the measles. All I could do over the next few days was sleep, drink fluids and listen to stories. I thought I had the flu!

Reading and Comprehension

1. The doctor told me I had
    (a) the flu.   (b) a cold.
    (c) the measles.   (d) school phobia.

2. Sports Day was on
    (a) Monday.
    (b) Wednesday.
    (c) the day after Thursday.
    (d) the weekend.

3. The measles can make you feel
    (a) full of energy.
    (b) hot and thirsty.
    (c) like you don't want to sleep.
    (d) happy.

4. Why wasn't Dad impressed with me?

    _____

5. Number these sentences in order (1–4).
    (a) The doctor told me it was measles.
    (b) My body was covered in spots.
    (c) I had to rest on the couch.
    (d) Matthew beat me at running.

Spelling and Vocabulary

Rewrite the misspelt words.

6. They sore Jason win the hopping race.

    _____

7. I shell complete my homework. _____

Circle the word that has the nearest meaning to the underlined word.

8. Dad caught a very large fish.
    (a) heavy
    (b) big
    (c) expensive
    (d) unique

9. Please start your homework!
    (a) begin
    (b) end
    (c) check
    (d) read

Circle the correct word in brackets.

10. My big sister went out (for, four) dinner.

11. Mum (new, knew) the way into town.

12. The book is heavier (then, than) the paperclips.

Grammar and Punctuation

13. Underline the **adjectives** in these sentences.

    Wash the red jumper in warm water. Hang to dry in a cool spot. Do not use a hot iron.

14. Punctuate and capitalise this sentence.

    im tired so im going to lie down on the couch

    _____

    _____

Number and Algebra

1.

+	15	19	20	1	0	21
0						

2.

−	11	21	16	8	12	20
1						

3.

×	9	6	13	20	15	50
0						

4. Write each number modelled as a numeral and in words.

(a) 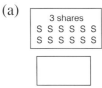 (b)

5. Write the next three numbers.

28, 38, 48, ☐ , ☐ , ☐

6. How many are in each share?

(a)
```
3 shares
S S S S S S
S S S S S S
```

(b)
```
5 shares
T T T T T
T T T T T
  T T T
```

7. Find four different ways to represent 30c.

1. ☐   2. ☐

3. ☐   4. ☐

Measurement and Geometry

8. What would the time be?

(a) 5 minutes before half past 12 ☐

(b) 20 minutes after a quarter past 10 ☐

9. One of Travis's shoes balanced 10 marbles. A book balanced 20 marbles. How many shoes would balance the book? ☐

10.

One metre	Half a metre	Quarter of a metre
X	Y	Z

In which column would each of these fit?

(a) the length of your ruler ☐

(b) the length of an adult's stride ☐

11. Does this shape tessellate? Explain your answer.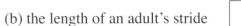

☐

12. Is each more than a litre, about a litre or less than a litre?

(a) water a bathtub can hold ☐

(b) soft drink a can holds ☐

13. Complete the rectangle by drawing in the missing lines. ☐

14. Complete the following.

(a) 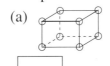 ☐ vertices

(b) ☐ vertex

15. 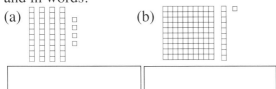 How many angles does this polygon have? ☐

16. How many lines of symmetry has a circle?

☐

Statistics and Probability

17. ⧂⧂⧂ = 5 lollies

How would you show 20 lollies?

☐

Note-taking challenge!

Indonesia is a close neighbour of ours. Read the notes made by one student in 3A during a silent reading session.

Indonesia:

- a tropical climate and is mainly covered in rainforest
- close to the equator and is north of Australia
- a busy industrial country which is made up of many islands
- many people involved in farming, forestry and factories
- crops—sugar, rice, coffee, tea, tobacco, rubber and sweet potato
- thriving fishing industry which exports a lot of shrimp
- endangered species include the Sumatran tiger, sun bear and elephant
- 1997 a devastating fire burnt out valuable timber, killed thousands of endangered animals and caused massive air pollution over a wide area
- grows fruits such as pawpaws, pineapples, oranges and melons
- popular sports such as soccer, badminton and table tennis are played.

Reading and Comprehension

1. The word *devastating* means
   (a) 'very destructive'.
   (b) 'causing floods'.
   (c) 'large-scale earthworks'.
   (d) 'of little importance'.

2. What are the fruits mentioned?

   _____

3. Which sports are played in Indonesia?

   _____

4. Which of these statements is true?
   (a) Indonesia has a number of endangered animals.
   (b) Indonesia is made up of a few large islands.
   (c) The country exports seafood.
   (d) Indonesia has a tropical climate and is close to the equator.

5. Apart from various fruits, which other crops are grown?

   _____

   _____

Spelling and Vocabulary

Rewrite the misspelt words.

6. I cryed all the way to school yesterday.

   _____

7. Milly had a dreem about giant mice.

   _____

Circle the word that has the nearest meaning to the underlined word.

8. We tried to post the letter before 4 o'clock.
   (a) stamp
   (b) mail
   (c) catch
   (d) open

9. Mum was on a fortnight's holiday.
   (a) six day
   (b) month's
   (c) two week
   (d) thirteen day

Circle the correct word in brackets.

10. (Wear, Where) are you going?

11. Sulu wanted to come (to, too).

12. Betty will (meat, meet) Sally at the school gate.

Grammar and Punctuation

13. Underline the **verbs** in these sentences.

    Add in the flour. Measure the milk. Mix to a soft paste. Bake in oven slowly.

14. Punctuate and capitalise this sentence.

    the girl was bitten on the knee by a redback spider

    _____

    _____

Number and Algebra

1. Follow this addition path.

6   +5   +2   +7   +4   +6   =

2. Help the painters go down the ladders. Each step represents <u>take away</u> one.

(a)   (b)   (c)   (d)

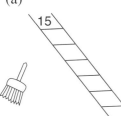  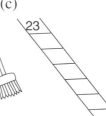 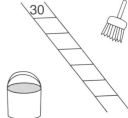

15   20   23   30

3. Complete the multiplication circles.

(a)   (b)   (c)

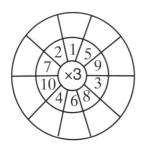 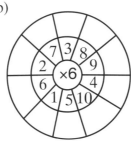 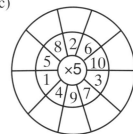

4. (a) What does the digit 4 mean in 48?

   (b) What does the digit 5 mean in 25?

   (c) How many times greater is 6 than 6 in 66?
          ○   □   ○□

   (d) How many ones are there in 19?

5. Cross out the number which does not belong in the following number patterns.

   (a) 2, 4, 6, 8, 10, 11, 12, 14, 16, 18   (b) 0, 5, 10, 15, 20, 21, 25, 30, 35, 40

   (c) 11, 12, 13, 14, 26, 15, 16, 17, 18, 19   (d) 7, 9, 11, 13, 15, 17, 18, 19, 21

6. What part is coloured?

7. Simon has two five-cent coins and three ten-cent coins in his pocket. How much money does he have?

Measurement and Geometry

8. Write the time as shown.

(a) **3 : 30** = | three | (b) **5 : 05** = | oh |

(c) **9 : 25** = | past | (d) **12 : 50** = | past |

9. Circle the heaviest object.

10. Pauline bought six metres of green ribbon. Alice bought only one metre of the same ribbon. How many more metres did Pauline buy?

11. How many small triangles have been used to cover this area?

12. Michael invited 20 people to his barbeque party. He bought 2 litres of orange juice for each of his guests. How many litres did he buy altogether?

13. Draw a square and colour it blue. Draw a pentagon and colour it red.

14. Name the shape in each cross-section.

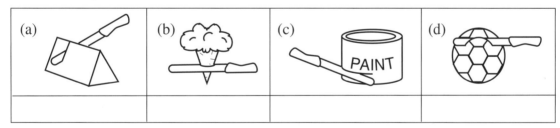

(a)	(b)	(c)	(d)

15. Draw an angle larger than a right angle. Use your pencil and ruler.

16. Study this square. Many lines of symmetry have been drawn in but one does not belong. Which one is not a line of symmetry?

Statistics and Probability

17. Anna graphed 10 domino picks. Which number came up the most?

4					
3					
5					
2					

Pet's day

Scene 1

Miss Wilson	Mrs Brown, do you know what I would like to do tomorrow for one of my lessons?
Mrs Brown	No, Miss Wilson. What?
Miss Wilson	I'd like to teach the children about caring and sharing. I think caring and sharing is so important, don't you?
Mrs Brown	Indeed I do. And how are you going to care and share in one half-hour lesson, might I ask?
Miss Wilson	Well, I have an idea. May I put it to the class?
Mrs Brown	You may. Listen, everyone. Miss Wilson has something important to say to us. Are you listening, Jeremy? Peter, get down from the top of that cupboard. Ready? Right, Miss Wilson.
Miss Wilson	Well, children, what's the most important thing to do if you have a pet?
Matthew	Teach it how to fight.
Miss Wilson	Well, not quite …
Wendy	Train it to eat the scraps.
Miss Wilson	That's not really what I meant.
Tran	Hit it on the nose with the newspaper if it wees on the carpet.
Miss Wilson	Er, yes. But we also have to c-c-c—
Georgi	Cut off its tail?
Miss Wilson	No, c-c-c—
Joe	Carry it around?
Miss Wilson	No. Well, it depends. What is your pet?
Joe	A horse.
Miss Wilson	No. We c-c-c—
Soula	Call it when it runs away?
Jeremy	Cash it in for money?
Miss Wilson	No. We have to c-c-*care*! Care for our pets. And we're going to learn to care for our pets at school.
Children	Ah! Ooh! Aahh!
Miss Wilson	Those of you who have pets can bring them to school tomorrow. Hands up how many people have pets. All of you! Oh …
Mrs Brown	I'm allergic to cat's fur.
Miss Wilson	Oh dear. And children, make sure your pets are in a box or on a lead.
Lucy	I've got a goldfish.
Miss Wilson	Or in a bowl. This will be lovely! We will learn about caring and sharing. Hands-on experience!
Mrs Brown	Hands *off* for me, I'm afraid. My allergies, remember.
Miss Wilson	Don't forget, children. Pet's Day tomorrow.

Scene 2

Miss Wilson	Good morning, Mrs Brown.
Mrs Brown	Good morning, Miss Wilson.
Miss Wilson	It's a lovely day to learn about caring and sharing, isn't it? And look, here are some children coming in already, so early— and the first bell hasn't even gone yet. They are so eager to care and share!
Mrs Brown	Er—yes …
Miss Wilson	Good morning, Matthew. And what have you got in that box?

From *Pet's Day* by Celeste Snowdon

Reading and Comprehension

1. Write the names of four children in the class.

   _____

   _____

2. Miss Wilson and Mrs Brown are probably
   (a) children.
   (b) teachers.
   (c) pets.
   (d) principals.

3. This play is set in a
   (a) playground.
   (b) pet shop.
   (c) park.
   (d) classroom.

4. What pet does Lucy have?
   (a) horse
   (b) goldfish
   (c) goat
   (d) cat

5. Number these sentences in order (1–4).
   (a) The children were reminded about Pet's Day.
   (b) Miss Wilson had an idea.
   (c) Mrs Brown has many allergies.
   (d) The teacher was asking lots of questions.

Spelling and Vocabulary

Rewrite the misspelt words.

6. Train it to eat the scrapes. _____

7. Pet's Day is tommorrow. _____

8. Write the plurals of these words.

   (a) pet   _____

   (b) child   _____

   (c) cat   _____

   (d) horse   _____

   (e) teacher   _____

   (f) fish   _____

Circle the word that has the nearest meaning to the underlined word.

9. I am <u>allergic</u> to the dust.
   (a) similar
   (b) related
   (c) addicted
   (d) sensitive

10. It will be a hands-on <u>experience</u>.
    (a) exercise
    (b) activity
    (c) expert
    (d) excitement

Circle the correct word in brackets.

11. Georgi said to cut off its (tail, tale).

12. Joe has a pet (hoarse, horse).

Grammar and Punctuation

13. Circle the **pronouns** in these sentences.

    I have a goldfish. We will learn about sharing and caring. Bring your pets. Are you allergic to anything?

14. These sentences are mixed up. Can you arrange them so that they make sense?

    has something / Miss Wilson / very important to say to us.

    _____

    _____

Number and Algebra

1.

+	17	12	15	20	19	18
8						

2.

–	16	20	25	19	31	36
6						

3.

×	5	10	0	7	2	12
4						

4. Write the numeral for two hundred and sixteen.

5. Complete the sequence:

42, 40, 38,

6. Give the fraction which is unshaded in this group.

sevenths

7. Match the group of coins to its value.

- $2.10
- $1.10
- $1.05
- $1.15

Measurement and Geometry

8. On each clockface show the time given.

10 o'clock   7 o'clock

9. If one ruler weighs about 20 nails, then

two rulers would weigh about [ ] nails.

 = ?

10. Would the height of an average door be about:
(a) 10 metres?
(b) 2 metres?
(c) 1 metre?

11. Colour the coin with the smallest surface.

(a)   (b)   (c)

12. Write these liquid measures the short way.

(a) one litre

(b) eight litres

(c) fifty-five litres

13. Give the names of the 3 plane shapes used to make this diagram.

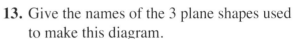

1.

2.

3.

14. In this table draw each face of the prism.

Prism	Shape of each face			
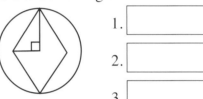	△			

15. How many square corners does this rectangle have? Mark them in blue.

16. A l __ __ __ of s __ __ __ __ t __ y divides something in half so that each half is a mirror image of the other.

Statistics and Probability

17.

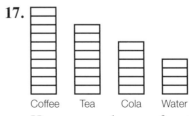

Coffee   Tea   Cola   Water

How many glasses of water and cola were consumed?

When Melissa Ann came to dinner

Just then the doorbell rang.

"Answer the door, Frances," my mother called.

A lady stood outside, smiling at me.

"Hello," she said. "Can I come in?"

It was Melissa Ann Grey.

"Justin's too busy," I said. "You'll have to come another day." I started to close the door.

"If Justin's too busy," Melissa Ann said, "may I visit you?"

I asked Melissa Ann if she knew how to play hide-and-seek. She told me she could hide so I would never find her.

"I'm a very good finder," I said.

"We'll see about that." Melissa Ann put her coat on the chair. She hid while I counted. Mum came out while I was counting.

"Who was at the door?" she said.

I told her it was Melissa Ann Grey.

"Where is she now?" Mum asked.

I told her I didn't know.

Mum looked puzzled. "She must be somewhere!"

"We've got to find her," I said.

Then Justin came running down the stairs. "Is Melissa Ann here?"

"Yes," I said. "She's hiding."

We all started looking for Melissa Ann. We looked upstairs and downstairs. We looked everywhere. But we couldn't find her.

Justin gave me a funny look. "You're only playing games with us, aren't you, Franny?"

"Yes, hide-and-seek!" I told him.

Just then Melissa Ann came into the room. "I told you I was good at hiding," she said.

From When Melissa Ann Came to Dinner by Dianne Bates

Reading and Comprehension

1. Who rang the doorbell?
   (a) Mum   (b) Justin
   (c) Franny   (d) Melissa

2. Melissa put her coat
   (a) in her bag.   (b) on the chair.
   (c) upstairs in Justin's room.
   (d) outside on the doorstep.

3. The other name used for Frances was

4. Why couldn't Justin play hide-and-seek at first?
   (a) He didn't like Melissa.
   (b) He didn't know how to play.
   (c) He was too busy.
   (d) His mother told him not to play.

5. Number these sentences in order (1–4).
   (a) It was Melissa Ann Grey.
   (b) Justin gave Frances a funny look.
   (c) Frances played hide-and-seek.
   (d) The doorbell rang.

Spelling and Vocabulary

Rewrite the misspelt words.

6. I mite be able to help you sell your bicycle.

7. Sheyd know if you were right or wrong.

Circle the word that has the nearest meaning to the underlined word.

8. We had a great day at the circus.
   (a) funny   (b) long   (c) fabulous   (d) tiring

9. Try not to rush your homework.
   (a) hurry   (b) ruin   (c) forget   (d) wreck

Circle the correct word in brackets.

10. Dad will be paid at the end of the (mouth, month).

11. The last (ferry, fairy) leaves at 5 o'clock.

12. The book was (cheep, cheap), so I bought it.

Grammar and Punctuation

13. Underline the **pronouns** in these sentences.

    I don't know if he invited Tom to his party. He said we were. My mum said I could go.

14. Punctuate and capitalise this sentence.

    welcome to freds funpark and remember to enjoy the rides

Number and Algebra

1.

+	10	20	30	40	50	60
9						

2.

–	30	20	10	90	70	80
8						

3.

÷	8	20	16	12	24	32
4						

4. Write the numeral for seven hundred.

5. (a) 180, 170, 160, ☐ , ☐ , ☐

(b) 80, 70, 60, ☐ , ☐ , ☐

(c) 83, 73, 63, ☐ , ☐ , ☐

6. Colour part of the group to match the fraction given: four-fifths.

7. Draw a group of notes with the same value as this one.

$50

Measurement and Geometry

8. What's the time now? ☐

12 : 06   3 minutes later it is: ☐ : ☐

9. Is this book heavier or lighter than a kilogram? ☐

10. Colour in the shorter tree.

(a)   (b)

11. How many ☐ are there in this block?

12. A coffee cup holds:

(a) less than a litre?

(b) about a litre?

(c) more than a litre?

13. Which shape below is a triangle? ☐

A B C D E F G H

14. Which picture shows a prism? ☐

(a)   (b)   (c)

CHOCOLATE

15. Name three places in your bedroom where you might find right angles.

1. ☐

2. ☐

3. ☐

16. Each shape below has been divided by a line of symmetry. Colour one half.

(a)   (b)

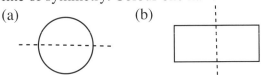

Statistics and Probability

17. cats 卌 |
dogs 卌 ||
mice |||

Favourite Pet

Complete the bar graph above.

Frogs

A frog is an amphibian. An adult frog has no tail. It has smooth skin and no hind legs. Their eggs are hatched in water. Female frogs can lay up to 1000 eggs—even more!

Baby frogs are called tadpoles. They have a tail and gills. Because they have gills, tadpoles stay underwater for long periods of time.

Frogs live on insects, worms and spiders. The capture of food is done by the frog's tongue which is covered in sticky stuff.

Anyone who brings a frog to school should be careful to wash their hands frequently as the sticky liquid is revolting. Just watch out that it doesn't get in your eyes or mouth.

Only male frogs croak. They have a sac of skin which can be inflated by air. You'll know if there is a bullfrog nearby!

Reading and Comprehension

1. Frogs belong to which animal family?
   (a) reptiles
   (b) amphibians
   (c) mammals
   (d) fish

2. Most frogs can stay under water for a long time because
   (a) they have no tail.
   (b) of the sticky stuff.
   (c) of their gills.
   (d) the bullfrogs look after them.

3. What part of the frog catches the food?
   (a) the sac
   (b) the tongue
   (c) the long hind legs
   (d) the gills

4. What are baby frogs called?

_____

5. Number these sentences in order (1–4).
   (a) Frogs eat insects.
   (b) Only male frogs croak.
   (c) A frog is an amphibian.
   (d) Tadpoles are baby frogs.

Spelling and Vocabulary

Rewrite the misspelt words.

6. I was told not to staye in the pool for too long.

_____

7. At the movies, there was a spare seet beside me.

_____

Circle the word from the list that has the nearest meaning to the underlined word.

8. Con had to wash away the dirt.
   (a) dish
   (b) peel
   (c) grime
   (d) rubbish

9. I have a thin layer of plastic on my book.
   (a) fine
   (b) thick
   (c) tidy
   (d) short

Circle the correct word in brackets.

10. Put (they, them) back where (they, them) belong.

11. This pencil is (mind, mine).

12. Only (to, too, two) children were able to leave early.

Grammar and Punctuation

13. Underline the **nouns** used in these sentences.

    A cylinder is a solid. It has no sides. It can roll. Cylinders have circular faces.

14. Punctuate and capitalise this sentence.

    hell bring the cheese butter eggs and flour

_____

_____

Number and Algebra

1.

+	20	30	45	15	5	50
20						

2.

–	13	23	33	43	53	63
10						

3.

×	0	1	5	2	6	10
5						

4. Write the numeral for three hundred and eight.

5. (a) 11, 13, 15, 17, ☐ , ☐ , ☐ , ☐

    (b) 130, 120, 110, ☐ , ☐ , ☐ , ☐

6. What fraction is coloured in this group?

 ☐ ninths

7. Match this group of notes to its correct value.

☐ $50   • $70
☐ $10   • $80
☐ $20   • $800
             • $78

Measurement and Geometry

8. On each face show the time given.
(a) 2 o'clock   (b) 9 o'clock

☐ :   ☐ :

9. Number these animals in order (1– 5) from the one you think has the least mass to the one you think has the greatest mass:

whale, rat, beetle, cow, cat

10. Colour the longest worm brown.
(a)   (b)   (c)

11. In which fan was the most paper used?
(a)   (b)   (c)

 ☐

12. Circle the one you think would hold the most water:

eggcup   wine bottle   tall
glass   large saucepan

13. How many plane shapes can you see in this diagram? ☐

14. Am I solid A, B or C?

A
B
C

• I have a curved surface.
• My ends are circles.
• I have no sides.

15. Draw a horizontal line 8 cm long.

16. Use 10 blocks and build two towers exactly the same size. Draw your models.

Statistics and Probability

17.

There are 4 apples on the shelf with a worm between each one. How many worms are there? ☐

Big April Fools!

It was breakfast time. When Miranda came into the kitchen, rubbing her eyes, Danny and Rose were already eating their cereal.

"Hi, sleepyhead", said Mum.

"Look out, Miranda", said Danny, pointing behind her. "There's a spider on the wall!"

Rose opened her eyes wide and took a quick, noisy breath. "Aark! A big, black, hairy one!" She shuddered.

Miranda turned quickly and looked.

"Where? I can't see it."

Danny laughed. "Ha, ha, ha! Big April Fool!"

Rose laughed, too.

"Don't be mean", said Dad. "Miranda hasn't been here long enough to know about April Fools' Day."

"Why didn't you explain yesterday?" said Mum. "It would have been a kind thing to do."

Miranda arrived from an orphanage in South America three months ago. She was learning to speak English. Mum said she was learning fast!

She was also learning about Australian holidays and celebrations.

Rose explained. "On April Fools' Day—in the morning—everyone plays tricks."

From Big April Fools! by Hazel Edwards

Reading and Comprehension

1. The April Fools' Day trick was played on
   (a) Rose.   (b) Mum.
   (c) Danny.   (d) Miranda.

2. Miranda had arrived from an orphanage in
   (a) Australia.   (b) South Africa.
   (c) South America. (d) South Australia.

3. Which one doesn't belong? Miranda was learning about
   (a) Australian celebrations.
   (b) English.
   (c) magic tricks.
   (d) Australian holidays.

4. How long had Miranda been here?

   _____

5. Number these sentences in order (1–4).
   (a) Dad told them not to be mean.
   (b) Miranda walked into the kitchen
   (c) There's a spider on the wall.
   (d) Everyone plays tricks on April Fools' Day.

Spelling and Vocabulary

Rewrite the misspelt words.

6. Do you know whether the cork can floaut?

   _____

7. Some thinks in my toybox need to be thrown out.

   _____

Circle the word that has the nearest meaning to the underlined word.

8. Pack your bags <u>early</u>!
   (a) beforehand   (b) late
   (c) slowly   (d) calmly

9. Anna tied the rope on a <u>strong</u> branch.
   (a) steady
   (b) lovely
   (c) thick
   (d) firm

Circle the correct word in brackets.

10. I (walk, walked) to the bank this morning.

11. I (talk, talked) to her on the phone an hour ago.

12. I (shout, shouted) the answer and was punished.

Grammar and Punctuation

13. Underline the **verbs** in these sentences.

    Take this flower. It smells beautiful. I love red flowers.

14. Punctuate and capitalise this sentence.

    do you know how to get to seymore street

    _____

    _____

Number and Algebra

1.

+	17	19	18	16	14	27
7						

2.

−	90	80	70	60	50	95
5						

3.

÷	30	40	50	60	70	75
5						

4. Write the numeral for six hundred and sixty.

5. Complete this number pattern.

25, 27, 29, ☐, ☐, ☐, ☐

6. Colour part of the group to match the fraction given—six-tenths

7. Draw a group of coins similar in value to this one.

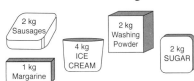

Measurement and Geometry

8. Draw lines to join the same times together.

5:30	three-thirty
12:30	half past five
3:30	30 minutes past 12

9. Which container is the lightest?

10. There are ☐ shorts in a metre.

11. How many blocks have been used to make this model?

12. Circle the one you think would hold the most sand:

teaspoon　　　　　kitchen sink

small bucket　　　flat cake dish

13. Match the shapes to the clues.

- oval
- semicircle
- circle

14. What shape will the cross-section be?

15. Draw a vertical line 2 cm long.

16. This net can be cut out and folded into which shape?

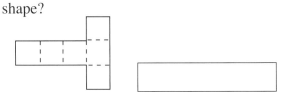

Statistics and Probability

17.

Roses 6	Daisies 4	Tulips 8

Construct a vertical bar graph to reflect the above information.

10			
9			
8			
7			
6			
5			
4			
3			
2			
1			

Kzot—the amazing robot

One night as I dreamed, tucked up in my bed
With all the blankets pulled over my head,
My silly dog Rufus started to bark;
He barked at something out there in the dark.
I crept to my window and quickly looked out;
I couldn't see anything moving about.
"Shush, Rufus", I said. "You know that's not right.
You musn't bark loudly, so late at night!"
Again I said, "Shush! You'll wake up Dad,
And my dad already thinks you're bad,
Cos you scratched a hole in the flyscreen door
And left a puddle on the loungeroom floor.
And why did you have to take his best shoe
Down to the backyard and give it a chew?"
"GOOD GRIEF!" I suddenly heard my dad snap.
"I'm tired of that wretched dog's endless yap!"
"That dog is a menace", I heard my dad shout.
"Now what on earth is it barking about?
It's twelve o'clock and we all need our rest.
Tomorrow—off to the pound with that pest!"
And then, I think, I was guided by fate
As I ran outside to investigate.
Something was moving, there in the grass—
Something that Rufus would not let pass.
I saw a contraption, not very high—it must have
fallen right out of the sky.
Something alien to the human race—perhaps it
had landed from outer space!

From *Kzot, the Amazing Robot* by Jan Weeks

Reading and Comprehension

1. The dog's name is
    (a) Shush.   (b) Cos.
    (c) Kzot.   (d) Rufus.

2. Why was the dog barking so much?
    (a) He was afraid of Dad.
    (b) He heard something moving.
    (c) He was scared of aliens.
    (d) He was going to the pound in the morning.

3. In the story, the word that rhymes with *snap* is
    (a) rap.   (b) slap.
    (c) Kzap.   (d) yap.

4. Find the word that means 'a pest'.

    _____

5. Number these sentences in order (1–4).
    (a) It looked like an alien.
    (b) I tucked myself in bed.
    (c) Rufus started barking.
    (d) I ran out to investigate.

Spelling and Vocabulary

Rewrite the misspelt words.

6. The dogs stood faic to faic. _____

7. Avery teacher at our school
    does playground duty. _____

Circle the word that has the nearest meaning to the underlined word.

8. Timmy <u>loves</u> eating strawberry ice-cream.
    (a) looks   (b) adores
    (c) likes   (d) hates

9. <u>Shine</u> your boots with this old rag.
    (a) stain   (b) shake
    (c) smell   (d) polish

Circle the correct word in brackets.

10. I saw the teenager go down the (road, rode).

11. The (smallest, small) plate is this one.

12. (Thing, Think) before you make up your mind!

Grammar and Punctuation

13. Underline the **adjectives** in these sentences.

    Bob has a deep voice. He is in the school
    choir. He is the boy with the red hat.

14. Punctuate and capitalise this sentence.

    i invited rebecca lisa soula and jane to
    waterworld

    _____

    _____

Number and Algebra

1.

+	17	18	19	20	21	27
3						

2.

–	21	46	53	70	25	31
2						

3.

÷	15	3	6	12	9	27
3						

4. Which numeral is shown on this numeral expander?

5. Write the next three numbers.

250, 240, 230, ☐ , ☐ , ☐

6.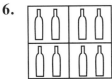

(a) How many groups are there? ☐

(b) How many are there in each group? ☐

(c) How many bottles are there altogether? ☐

7. What is the value of this caterpillar? ☐

Measurement and Geometry

8. Write the time shown.

(a)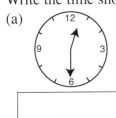

(b)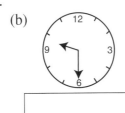

☐   ☐

9. The object I have has a mass of about two kilograms. Which one is it?

(a)   (b)    (c)

10. The object I have has a length of three centimetres. Which one would it be?

(a)   (b)   (c)

11. Calculate the area of this shape.

12.

13. How many squares make up the robot? 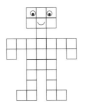 ☐

14. Fill in the missing letters.

r _ _ _ a _ _ ul _ _   _ _ _ s _

15. An angle is the amount of _ _ _ _ between two arms.

16. Have we used **flip**, **slide** or **turn** to make this coloured shape? ☐

Statistics and Probability

17.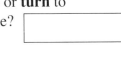

Carton 3 L   Bowl 4 L   Jug 1 L   Bottle 2 L

Which container holds the most fluid? ☐

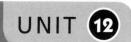

Simpson and Duffy

A long time ago there lived a man and a donkey. The man's name was John Simpson Kirkpatrick and he was a soldier in the Australian Army. He went to war at a place called Gallipoli in Turkey. Gallipoli is near the sea and has steep cliffs.

Simpson worked with the Medical Corps. He was a stretcher bearer. His job was to go to the battlefields and bring back the injured soldiers to the first aid station. The track down the cliff was long, winding and dangerous.

John Simpson loved animals and one morning he found a donkey, alone and scared of the terrible war noises.

"You will be my helper", said Simpson. "I will call you Duffy. We can carry the wounded soldiers down from the battlefield."

Many times a day and during the night, Duffy and Simpson walked together up and down the dusty track in the boiling sun. It was tiring for them and the other soldiers thought they were very brave. Sadly, one morning, the fighting was worse than usual. A hail of enemy bullets shot Simpson through the heart. Duffy continued his journey down to the medical station, alone.

From *Simpson and Duffy* by Mary Small

Reading and Comprehension

1. What job in the Army did Simpson have?
   (a) Captain (b) patient
   (c) animal carer (d) stretcher bearer

2. Where is Gallipoli?
   (a) Australia (b) Melbourne
   (c) Turkey (d) Greece

3. How did Simpson die?
   (a) He was fighting a soldier.
   (b) He had to chase after Duffy.
   (c) The heat was too much.
   (d) He was shot.

4. How did the donkey assist John Simpson?

   _____

5. Number these sentences in order (1–4).
   (a) He found a donkey.
   (b) He was shot.
   (c) John Simpson was a stretcher bearer.
   (d) They carried the hurt soldiers.

Spelling and Vocabulary

Rewrite the misspelt words.

6. The farmer fell asleep in the staple.

   _____

7. Kim road to my place on a motorbike.

   _____

Circle the word that has the nearest meaning to the underlined word.

8. Keep your cough medicine in the fridge.
   (a) kick (b) hold
   (c) rest (d) cool

9. The tiny baby was only 45 cm long.
   (a) little (b) young
   (c) large (d) nice

Circle the correct word in brackets.

10. His teacher (took, take) the toys away.

11. (Them, These) shoes belong to my baby brother.

12. I had to (peeling, peel) the potatoes for Mum.

Grammar and Punctuation

13. Underline the **pronouns** in these sentences.

    They did not know what to do. I explained it to them. She didn't thank me. I was hurt.

14. Punctuate and capitalise this sentence.

    robin hill is now a member of the tigers' netball team

    _____

    _____

Number and Algebra

1.

+	5c	10c	25c	50c	95c	$1
5c						

2.

−	10c	80c	5c	20c	$1	75c
5c						

3.

×	10	6	5	7	0	20
2						

4. Write the numeral for:

(a) seventy

(b) seventeen

5. Write the next three numbers.

92, 94, 96, ☐ , ☐ , ☐

6. What part is coloured?

(a)   (b)

7. What is the change from $2 if I buy a milkshake worth $1.15?

Measurement and Geometry

8. Use lines to join the same times.
daybreak   12:00
midnight   6:00
afternoon   3:00

9. The object I have has a mass of one kilogram. Which one is it?

(a)   (b)   (c)

ONIONS 5 kg

10. The object I have has a length of three metres. Which one is it?

(a)   (b)   (c)

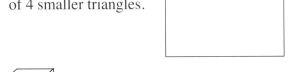

11. Draw a triangle made up of 4 smaller triangles.

12.

5 L − 1 L = ☐ L

13. Colour and count all the circles.

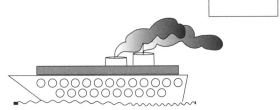

14. Name the solid shape that has flat and curved surfaces. Draw it.

15. Which angle is the sharpest?

Q   R   S

16. True or False?
We used a **slide** to make the coloured shape.

Statistics and Probability

17.

How many spaces are there between the hearts?

Label it!

1

Washing Instructions

Wash in lukewarm water with mild soap or detergent. Do not wring or twist.

Use cool iron (NOT HOT) on the back side of garment.

2

DRY CLEANING RECOMMENDED

3

GLIDO
RELIEVES DISTRESS OF COLDS
Rub on throat, chest and back
Made in Australia

4

GLUE POP
Instant Drying
• Safe
• Non-toxic
• Ideal for paper use in the home and school

5

COVERO
Just for Kids

Kid Size Strips for cuts and bruises...

Directions: Apply bandage to clean, dry skin.
Change when it gets wet!

50 (2 × 6 cm)

6

WARNING
Keep out of reach of children
GLUE CRAFT
For sticking wood · plastic · material · paper
500 mL

Reading and Comprehension

1. Label 3 tells you that
   (a) it is a strong glue.
   (b) it needs a cool iron.
   (c) it is made in Australia.
   (d) the material might catch fire easily.

2. Read Label 5. How many bandages are there in the packet?
   (a) 500   (b) 50   (c) 2   (d) 6

3. If you saw Label 1 on a shirt, you would
   (a) put it in the spin-dryer.
   (b) use a hot iron only.
   (c) wash it in plenty of soap.
   (d) gently wash it in warm water.

4. Which of the glue labels warns you that children should not use it?

   _____

5. Look at Label 1 and number these sentences in order (1–4).
   (a) Iron on other side.
   (b) Do not wring or twist.
   (c) Wash in warm water.
   (d) Use a cool iron only.

Spelling and Vocabulary

Rewrite the misspelt words.

6. We were asked to stand stil at Assembly.

   _____

7. Fred took a bite out of the apple and it was sower.

   _____

Circle the word(s) with the nearest meaning to the underlined word.

8. I know that I can always <u>trust</u> Grandma.
   (a) treasure   (b) speak
   (c) tell   (d) rely on

9. My sick budgie looked a bit <u>frail</u>.
   (a) weak
   (b) fat
   (c) rib
   (d) fearful

Circle the correct word in brackets.

10. The wind (blew, blue) very strongly.

11. He (sat, set) in the back-seat of the car.

12. He did (not, note) know how to do the problem.

Grammar and Punctuation

13. Underline the **adjectives** in these sentences.

    I walked into the quiet room. My heavy breathing scared him. Up jumped my baby brother!

14. Punctuate and capitalise this sentence.

    you're invited to my birthday party on saturday 12th october

    _____

    _____

Number and Algebra

1.

+	7	8	9	10	11	17
7						

2.

−	20	19	18	17	16	23
4						

3.

×	1	10	3	2	5	6
6						

4. Write the numeral for four hundred and twenty-nine.

5. Complete the sequence: 229, 230, 231,

☐ , ☐ , ☐ , ☐

6. Share the lollies so that each basket has an equal share.

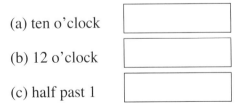

7. What is the total savings in the piggybank?

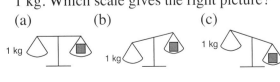

50c 10c 50c

Measurement and Geometry

8. Write the following times in digital time.

(a) ten o'clock ☐

(b) 12 o'clock ☐

(c) half past 1 ☐

9. The object I have has a mass of more than 1 kg. Which scale gives the right picture?

(a)   (b)   (c)

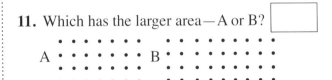

1 kg   1 kg   1 kg

10. Simon's pencil is about:

(a) 50 cm long?

(b) 15 cm long?

(c) 3 cm long? ☐

11. Which has the larger area—A or B? ☐

A   B

12. Number the volume of each carton (1–3) from smallest to largest.

(a)   (b)   (c)

CORNIES FAMILY SIZE   CORNIES JUMBO SIZE   CORNIES MINI SIZE

13. Which of these shapes is a rhombus? ☐

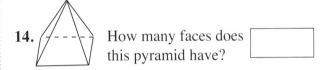

A   B   C   D   E   F

14.  How many faces does this pyramid have? ☐

15. Which angle is smaller—A or B? ☐

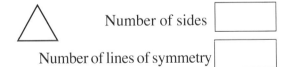

A   B

16. Study the triangle below.

Number of sides ☐

Number of lines of symmetry ☐

Statistics and Probability

17. ✓ ✓ ✓ ✗ ● ✗ ✗ ● ● ● ✓ ✓ ✓ ✓ ✓ ✓ ✓

Draw blocks to show how many ticks there are.

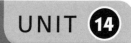
Greetings from the Great Barrier Reef!

Hi Nan! Hi Pop!

We're having a great time here. The weather's been beautiful. Haven't had any rain but the nights have been a bit chilly. On Saturday, we took a boat ride out to Green Island. I had my first tropical smorgasbord but I think I overdid it on the prawns! We stayed there for a few hours and later on I got to do some snorkelling. The fish were so colourful and a stingray passed right in front of me. Mum had a headache—she said it was the wine so she went back to the hut and did her nails! I liked the jet skiing the best. It was cool! Dad had his first taste of lobster, but I wasn't allowed to have any. Boo hoo!

I bought you a pretty shell necklace and Pop a funny T-shirt. Miss you both. Tomorrow we're off to Lizard Island. Dad said we're going on a glass-bottomed boat and afterwards we are going fishing on the Reef. Did I tell you that I miss you both? Be back Thursday. Pat Rex for me. I love him and coconut milkshakes!

See ya!

Wendy

(P.S. Did you know that a newly born crocodile is three times the size of its egg?)

Reading and Comprehension

1. The first thing Wendy did was
    (a) go fishing.   (b) go snorkelling.
    (c) go jet skiing.   (d) go on a boat ride.

2. Why didn't her mother go snorkelling?
    (a) She was fishing.
    (b) She went shopping.
    (c) She was eating lobster.
    (d) She had a headache.

3. How do you know that Wendy loves her grandparents very much?
    (a) She bought them something.
    (b) She wrote them a postcard.
    (c) She said that she missed them—twice.
    (d) She let them have Rex.

4. What is a tropical smorgasbord? Explain it in your own words.

    _____

    _____

5. Number these sentences in order (1–4).
    (a) Dad tasted lobster.
    (b) The weather is beautiful.
    (c) Mum had a headache.
    (d) We are going to Lizard Island.

Spelling and Vocabulary

Rewrite the misspelt words.

6. Margaret noticed a black spot on your dog's tale. _____

7. I started to tare the pieces of paper.

    _____

Circle the word that has the nearest meaning to the underlined word.

8. Helping me was a <u>kind</u> thing to do.
    (a) good   (b) nice
    (c) ripe   (d) great

9. "<u>Colour</u> the rivers in blue," said my teacher.
    (a) cut   (b) shade
    (c) glue   (d) cover

Circle the correct word in brackets.

10. He (knelt, kneel) down beside the bed.

11. The cat (hide, hid) from the dogs.

12. My friend (stood, stand) in the doorway.

Grammar and Punctuation

13. Underline the **nouns** in these sentences.

    I've been to Italy, Greece, France and Spain. One day, I hope to go to China.

14. Punctuate and capitalise this sentence.

    melbourne is the capital of victoria

    _____

    _____

Number and Algebra

1.
+	20	4	0	12	9	24
4						

2.
–	10	7	14	15	20	17
7						

3.
÷	10	17	100	1	2	57
1						

4. Write the numeral for:

5. Complete the sequence: 102, 101, 100,

☐ , ☐ , ☐ , ☐

6. One-half of the bananas are ripe.
How many are green?

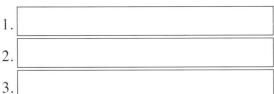

7. How many
20c coins equal
this coin? $2

Measurement and Geometry

8. List 3 things which take about 5 minutes to do:

1.
2.
3.

9. Does the watermelon weigh more or less than the mass?

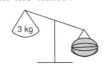

10. Make a list of 3 things which measure about 1 cm.

1.
2.
3.

11. Draw a square that is made up of four smaller squares.

12. Arrange these containers in order of capacity.

(a)   (b)   (c)   (d)   (e)

13. Cross out the quadrilaterals.

14. How many edges does this pyramid have?

15. Circle the right-angled triangle.

16. Slide this flag to the left 3 times.

Statistics and Probability

17. Draw 12 ice-creams in a row.

How many spaces are there?

An acrostic poem

Jason is from Sydney. He is now living on Thursday Island in the Torres Straits. He decided to write an acrostic poem on the Torres Straits.

Torres Strait islanders just love music!

Ornate headdresses are often worn when dancing.

Rattles for dance are often made out of shells or nuts.

Reefs of coral abound in this area.

Earth ovens are often used to cook food.

Seafaring people from northern Australia.

Seaman Dan is a famous singer from the area.

There are over one hundred islands in the strait.

Right next to Australia is where the islands are located.

Around the volcanic soil, yams and coconuts are grown.

Islanders hunt for turtles and dugongs.

Traditional singing and dancing are part of special feasts.

Surrounding warm seas contain a variety of fish.

Reading and Comprehension

1. The word *ornate* means
   (a) 'bright and shiny'.
   (b) 'highly decorated'.
   (c) 'blue and green'.
   (d) 'old and well-worn'.

2. The third letter in the acrostic refers to
   (a) climate.
   (b) turtles.
   (c) coconuts
   (d) dancing gear.

3. What are the two food plants mentioned?
   _____

4. Label the sentences **true** or **false**.
   (a) There are over 100 islands in the Torres Straits area. _____
   (b) The islands are just north of Australia. _____
   (c) The Torres Strait islanders are a seafaring people. _____

5. What are the sea creatures that the islanders hunt for food?
   _____

Spelling and Vocabulary

Rewrite the misspelt words.

6. Here I come, reddy or not! _____

7. Dad always helps Mum carrie the groceries.
   _____

Circle the word that has the nearest meaning to the underlined word.

8. If you swing on it you'll <u>break</u> it!
   (a) bear   (b) brush
   (c) dirty   (d) damage

9. Hot water can badly <u>burn</u> your skin.
   (a) bleed   (b) scorch
   (c) bruise   (d) storm

Circle the correct word in brackets.

10. Put this (book, look) back on the shelf.

11. This drink is far too (sweet, sweat) for me.

12. I am (played, playing) with my new friend.

Grammar and Punctuation

13. Underline the **verbs** in these sentences.

    Brush your teeth after every meal. Wash your mouth too. Tear a small piece of floss and use it.

14. Punctuate and capitalise this sentence.

    mr braldo has just arrived at mount more state school

    _____

    _____

Number and Algebra

1. Follow this addition path.

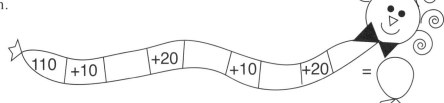

110 +10   +20   +10   +20   =

2. Complete:

(a)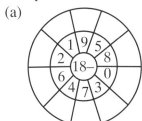

(b)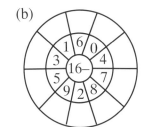

(c)

3. Complete these multiplication grids.

(a)

×	3	6	2	9	4	7	5	8	10
2									
4									

(b)

×	6	3	7	2	10	4	8	5	9
5									
10									

4. Write the numeral for the number shown on each abacus.

(a)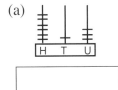

(b)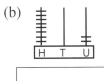

(c)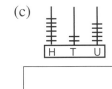

(d)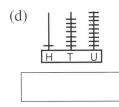

5. Complete the number pattern.

105 110 115

6. (a) Colour a fifth of the forks.

   (b) How many ticks are **not** coloured? ☐
   ✓ ✓ ✓ ✓ ✓ ✓ ✓ ✓ ✓

7. Let's go shopping! You have $1. Can you afford to buy:

 90c   20c   50c   70c   10c

(a) a toy car? ☐   (b) a balloon? ☐   (c) two balloons? ☐

(d) five combs? ☐   (e) a drink and a balloon? ☐   (f) three icecreams? ☐

(g) two drinks? ☐   (h) a toy car and a comb? ☐

Answers

Maths

1. 8, 10, 11, 12, 14, 15
2. 2, 4, 3, 9, 11, 20
3. 5, 3, 8, 6, 9, 12
4. 69
5. 50, 60, 70, 80, 90
6. quarters
7. 20 cents
8. 6:17
9. b, c, e and f
10. 2 m
11. 20
12. 8 cups
13.
14. cube
15. angle (a)
16. (a)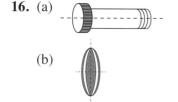
    (b)

17. (a) 3   (b) 2

English

1. b
2. d
3. c
4. d
5. 1c, 2a, 3d, 4b
6. breakfast
7. centimetre
8. a
9. c
10. there
11. soul
12. would
13. go, jumps, soil
14. The town of Broken Hill is in New South Wales.

Maths

1. 6, 3, 11, 8, 13, 19
2. 2, 8, 10, 4, 7, 11
3. 2, 4, 7, 1, 3, 6
4. 102
5. (a) 35, 40, 45
    (b) 75, 70, 65
6. (a) a half   (b) a fourth
7. 50c and 5c
8. (a) 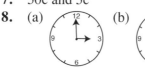   (b)

9. b, c and d
10. (a) 3 cm   (b) 4 cm
    (c) 1 cm
11. 4
12.

13. rectangle and triangle
14. ball, candle, glass, tin
15. oval
16. parent/teacher check
17. 6

English

1. c
2. c
3. d
4. Pandas do not hibernate, bamboo stays green even when there are metres of snow on the ground.
5. 1c, 2a, 3d, 4b
6. harm
7. scratch
8. d
9. b
10. won
11. ate
12. one
13. father, Dad, hair, teeth, eyes
14. For lunch, I had a piece of fish and some chips with tomato sauce.

Maths

1. 18, 14, 17, 8, 13, 24
2. 2, 0, 3, 7, 1, 21
3. 10, 16, 6, 14, 8, 24
4. 444
5. (a) 51, 61, 71, 81
    (b) 96, 95, 94, 93
6. (a) (b)

7. 30 cents
8. 2:30 (30 minutes past 2), 10:30 (half past 10), 8:30 (eight thirty)
9. (a) 95 kg   (b) 102 kg
    (c) 22 kg
10. answers will vary
11. 9 squares
12. about 40
13. 10 triangles, 6 circles
14. rectangular prism, sphere, cone, cylinder, cube
15. right angle
16. cheese stick, bread, banana
17. 18

English

1. a
2. **d**
3. d
4. **the rain**
5. 1b, 2c, 3d, 4a
6. bleed
7. pour
8. c
9. a
10. buy
11. sale
12. By
13. my, she, her
14. The thief ran out of Peter's Pizzeria and straight into a bin.

Answers

UNIT **4** page 14

Maths

1. 17, 10, 15, 20, 11, 25
2. 1, 0, 6, 10, 8, 20
3. 10, 15, 20, 2, 0, 30
4. 312
5. (a) 51, 41, 31
   (b) 402, 502, 602
6. (a) (b)

7. (a) 1, 61 (b) 1, 97
   (c) 0, 58
8. (a) 47, 8 (b) 59, 5
9. 5 kg, 50 kg, 500 kg, 505 kg, 550 kg
10. 5 m
11. 12 triangles
12. 11 blocks
13. (a) 8 cm (b) 1 cm
14. (a) cone
    (b) triangular prism
    (c) rectangular prism
15. parent/teacher check
16. 5
17. 17

English

1. b
2. a
3. d
4. about 30 minutes
5. 1d, 2a, 3c, 4b
6. balloon
7. ramp
8. b
9. c
10. allowed
11. bite
12. blue
13. Susan, piano, Monday, mum, guitar
14. The capital of Queensland is Brisbane.

UNIT **5** page 16

Maths

1. 17, 27, 37, 47, 57, 77
2. 3, 13, 23, 33, 43, 63
3. 2, 4, 6, 8, 10, 12
4. 463
5. 35, 25, 15
6. a half (or four eighths)
7. 70 cents
8. parent/teacher check
9. (a) 2 kg (b) 3 kg
   (c) 75 kg
10. (a)
    (b)
    (c)
11. (a) 35 squares
    (b) 9 squares
12. answers will vary
13. (a) circle
    (b) diamond or square
    (c) rectangle
14.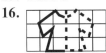
15. a and d
16.
17. (a) 5
    (b) dots

English

1. d
2. c
3. c
4. none
5. 1a, 2c, 3d, 4b
6. brought
7. cupboard
8. c
9. b
10. tied
11. flower
12. been
13. they, she, he, it, we
14. I bought some roses and carnations for Mrs Molly.

UNIT **6** page 18

Maths

1. 18, 19, 9, 17, 14, 21
2. 0, 5, 9, 7, 1, 10
3. 30, 20, 40, 70, 10, 100
4. (a) 211 (b) 107
5. 16, 14, 12, 10
6. (a)

7. (a) 90 cents (b) 20 cents
   (c) $1.60
8. (a) 4/1/86 or 04.01.86
   (b) 26/6/98 or 26.06.98
9. (a) softball
   (b) answers will vary
   (c) chair
10. (a) more than (b) more than
    (c) less than
11. 10
12. (a) about 4 cups
    (b) answers will vary
13. (a) 3 (b) 3
    (c) 5 (d) 5
14. (a) cone (b)
    (c)
15. parent/teacher check
16.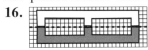

17. (a) +
    (b) 10

English

1. c   2. b
3. b
4. I played dot-to-dot with my spots.
5. 1c, 2d, 3b, 4a
6. saw   7. shall
8. b   9. a
10. for   11. knew
12. than
13. red, warm, cool, hot
14. I'm tired so I'm going to lie down on the couch.

Answers

Maths

1. 15, 19, 20, 1, 0, 21
2. 10, 20, 15, 7, 11, 19
3. 0, 0, 0, 0, 0, 0
4. (a) 44, forty-four
   (b) 111, one hundred and eleven
5. 58, 68, 78
6. (a) 4   (b) 3
7. 10c + 10c + 10c; 20c + 10c; 20c + 5c + 5c; 5c + 5c + 5c + 5c + 5c +5c; 10c + 10c + 5c + 5c
8. (a) 12:25   (b) 10:35
9. 2
10. (a) Y   (b) X
11. no, there are gaps between the circles
12. (a) more than   (b) less than
13. [diagram of a rectangle with dashed bottom edge]
14. (a) 8   (b) 1
15. 6
16. an infinite (endless) number
17. [candy/sweet pattern symbols]

English

1. a
2. pawpaws, pineapples, oranges and melons
3. soccer, badminton, table tennis
4. true, false, true, true
5. sugar, rice, coffee, tea, tobacco, rubber, sweet potato
6. cried
7. dream
8. b
9. c
10. where
11. too
12. meet
13. add, measure, mix, bake
14. The girl was bitten on the knee by a redback spider.

Maths

1. $6 + 5 = 11 + 2 = 13 + 7$
   $= 20 + 4 = 24 + 6 = 30$
2. (a) 15, 14, 13, 12, 11, 10, 9
   (b) 20, 19, 18, 17, 16, 15, 14
   (c) 23, 22, 21, 20, 19, 18, 17
   (d) 30, 29, 28, 27, 26, 25, 24
3. (a)   (b)

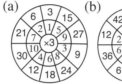

   (c)

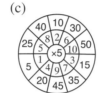

4. (a) 40 or 4 tens
   (b) 5 ones or 5
   (c) 10 times bigger
   (d) 19 ones (9 ones in one place)
5. (a) 11   (b) 21
   (c) 26   (d) 18
6. one-fourth (or a quarter)
7. 40 cents
8. (a) three-thirty
   (b) five-oh-five
   (c) twenty-five past nine
   (d) fifty past twelve
9. 5 kg potatoes
10. 5 metres
11. 24 triangles
12. 40 litres
13. parent/teacher check
14. (a) triangle (b) circle
    (c) circle   (d) circle
15. parent/teacher check
16. C
17. 5

English

1. Matthew, Wendy, Tran, Georgi, Joe, Soula, Jeremy, Lucy or Peter
2. b
3. d
4. b
5. 1b, 2d, 3c, 4a
6. scraps
7. tomorrow
8. (a) pets
   (b) children
   (c) cats
   (d) horses
   (e) teachers
   (f) fish
9. d
10. b
11. tail
12. horse
13. I, we, your, you
14. Miss Wilson has something very important to say to us.

Answers

UNIT 8 page 26

Maths

1. 25, 20, 23, 28, 27, 26
2. 10, 14, 19, 13, 25, 30
3. 20, 40, 0, 28, 8, 48
4. 216
5. 36, 34, 32, 30
6. six sevenths
7. $1.15
8. (a) (b)
9. about 40 nails
10. b
11. b
12. (a) 1 L (b) 8 L
    (c) 55 L
13. circle, diamond, triangle
    (right angled)
14.
15. 4 corners
16. line of symmetry
17. 10

English

1. d
2. b
3. Franny
4. c
5. 1d, 2a, 3c, 4b
6. might
7. she'd
8. c
9. a
10. month
11. ferry
12. cheap
13. I, he, his, he, we, my, I
14. Welcome to Fred's Funpark
    and remember to enjoy the
    rides!

UNIT 9 page 28

Maths

1. 19, 29, 39, 49, 59, 69
2. 22, 12, 2, 82, 62, 72
3. 2, 5, 4, 3, 6, 8
4. 700
5. (a) 150, 140, 130
   (b) 50, 40, 30
   (c) 53, 43, 33
6.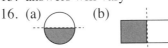
7. parent/teacher check
8. 6 past 12, 12:09
9. lighter
10. a
11. 100
12. less than
13. D
14. c
15. answers will vary
16. (a) (b)
17.

Favourite Pet						
cats						
dogs						
mice						

English

1. b
2. c
3. b
4. tadpoles
5. 1c, 2d, 3a, 4b
6. stay
7. seat
8. c
9. a
10. them, they
11. mine
12. two
13. cylinder, solid, sides,
    cylinders, faces
14. He'll bring the cheese,
    butter, eggs and flour.

UNIT 10 page 30

Maths

1. 40, 50, 65, 35, 25, 70
2. 3, 13, 23, 33, 43, 53
3. 0, 5, 25, 10, 30, 50
4. 308
5. (a) 19, 21, 23, 25
   (b) 100, 90, 80, 70
6. two-ninths
7. $80
8. (a) 2:00 (b) 9:00
9. 1-beetle, 2-rat, 3-cat, 4-cow,
   5-whale
10. c
11. a
12. large saucepan
13. 9
14. B
15. parent/teacher check
16.
17. 3

English

1. d
2. c
3. c
4. 3 months
5. 1b, 2c, 3a, 4d
6. float
7. things
8. a
9. d
10. walked
11. talked
12. shouted
13. take, smells, love
14. Do you know how to get to
    Seymore Street?

Answers

UNIT 11 page 32

Maths

1. 24, 26, 25, 23, 21, 34
2. 85, 75, 65, 55, 45, 90
3. 6, 8, 10, 12, 14, 15
4. 660
5. 31, 33, 35, 37
6.
7. answers will vary
8. 5:30 (half past five),
   12:30 (30 minutes past 12),
   3:30 (three-thirty)
9. 1 kg margarine
10. 100 shorts
11. 9 blocks
12. kitchen sink
13. circle, oval, semi-circle
14. circle
15. parent/teacher check
16. cube
17.

10				
9				
8		▓		
7		▓		
6	▓	▓		
5	▓	▓		
4	▓	▓		
3	▓	▓		
2	▓	▓		
1	▓	▓		
	Roses	Daisies	Tulips	

English

1. d
2. b
3. d
4. menace
5. 1b, 2c, 3d, 4a
6. face-to-face
7. Every
8. b
9. d
10. road
11. smallest   12. Think
13. deep, school, red
14. I invited Rebecca, Lisa, Soula
    and Jane to Waterworld.

UNIT 12 page 34

Maths

1. 20, 21, 22, 23, 24, 30
2. 19, 44, 51, 68, 23, 29
3. 5, 1, 2, 4, 3, 9
4. 82
5. 220, 210, 200
6. (a) 4
   (b) 2
   (c) 8
7. 95 cents
8. (a) 12:30
   (b) 9:30
9. c
10. b
11. 10 squares
12. 3 L
13. 30 squares
14. rectangular prism
15. turn
16. flip
17. Bowl

English

1. d
2. c
3. d
4. The donkey carried the
   wounded soldiers.
5. 1c, 2a, 3d, 4b
6. stable
7. rode
8. b
9. a
10. took
11. These
12. peel
13. they, I, them, it, she, me, I
14. Robin Hill is now a member
    of the Tigers' netball team.

UNIT 13 page 36

Maths

1. 10c, 15c, 30c, 55c, $1, $1.05
2. 5c, 75c, 0c, 15c, 95c, 70c
3. 20, 12, 10, 14, 0, 40
4. (a) 70   (b) 17
5. 98, 100, 102
6. (a) five fifths (a whole)
   (b) one fourth (one quarter)
7. 85c
8. daybreak (6:00), midnight
   (12:00), afternoon (3:00)
9. c
10. c
11.
12. 4 L
13. 23 circles
14. cylinder or cone

15. angle S
16. true
17. 6

English

1. c
2. b
3. d
4. Label 6
5. 1c, 2b, 3d, 4a
6. still
7. sour
8. d
9. a
10. blew
11. sat
12. not
13. quiet, heavy, baby
14. You're invited to my
    birthday party on Saturday,
    12th October.

Answers

UNIT 14 page 38

Maths

1. 14, 15, 16, 17, 18, 24
2. 16, 15, 14, 13, 12, 19
3. 6, 60, 18, 12, 30, 36
4. 429
5. 232, 233, 234, 235
6. 3 lollies each
7. $1.10
8. (a) 10:00
   (b) 12:00
   (c) 1:30
9. c
10. b
11. B
12. 1c, 2a, 3b
13. D
14. 5 faces
15. A
16. (a) 3
    (b) 3
17.

English

1. d
2. d
3. c
4. answers will vary
5. 1b, 2c, 3a, 4d
6. tail
7. tear
8. b
9. b
10. knelt
11. hid
12. stood
13. Italy, Greece, France, Spain, day, China
14. Melbourne is the capital of Victoria.

UNIT 15 page 40

Maths

1. 24, 8, 4, 16, 13, 28
2. 3, 0, 7, 8, 13, 10
3. 10, 17, 100, 1, 2, 57
4. 314
5. 99, 98, 97, 96
6. 4
7. 10 coins
8. answers will vary
9. more
10. answers will vary
11.
12. b, e, a, d, c
13.
14. 8 edges
15.
16.
17.
    11

English

1. b
2. d
3. yams, coconuts
4. true, true, true
5. turtles, dugong
6. ready
7. carry
8. d
9. b
10. book
11. sweet
12. playing
13. brush, wash, tear, use
14. Mr Braldo has just arrived at Mount More State School.

TEST 2 page 42

Maths

1. 110 + 10 = 120 + 20 = 140 + 10 = 150 + 20 = 170
2. (a)   (b)

   (c)

3. (a) 6, 12, 4, 18, 8, 14, 10, 16, 20
       and
       12, 24, 8, 36, 16, 28, 20, 32, 40
   (b) 30, 15, 35, 10, 50, 20, 40, 25, 45
       and
       60, 30, 70, 20, 100, 40, 80, 50, 90
4. (a) 613   (b) 802
   (c) 625   (d) 179
5. 105, 110, 115, 120, 125, 130, 135, 140, 145, 150, 155
6. (a) colour 1 fork
   (b) four tenths
7. (a) yes   (b) yes
   (c) yes   (d) yes
   (e) no   (f) yes
   (g) no   (h) yes
8. (a) 10:00   (b) 6:00
   (c) 1:30   (d) 3:00
9. 4 kg of fruit
10. (a) more   (b) about
    (c) less   (d) less
11. 17 blocks
12. (a) 6   (b) 8
    (c) 4   (d) 7
13. a
14. sphere, cone, cube, pyramid, cylinder, rectangular prism
15. angle B
16. A-turn, B-slide, C-flip
17. chips

Answers

English

1. c
2. d
3. c
4. mate or pal
5. 1c, 2d, 3a, 4b
6. helped
7. ten
8. wood
9. Their
10. (a) deep
    (b) boy
    (c) him
11. c
12. a
13. Errol, boy, pals, ambulance, hospital, examination
14. Errol Anseley is from Frenchs Forest and he was hauled from a four-metre pit.

Maths

1. 51, 63, 79, 54, 90, 100
2. 89, 56, 87, 42, 69, 70
3. 24, 68, 38, 43, 77, 99
4. 364
5. 184, 194, 204
6. 3, 4
7. $1.50 (150c)
8. Tuesday
9. Tim
10. rule a line (10 cm), jumping race (100 m), throw a ball (10 m)
11. 12 squares
12. 30 L
13. ◯
14. D, all others are solid shapes, a rectangle is a plane shape
15. (a) [clock face] (b) right angle
16. both squares have 4 lines of symmetry
17. Tuesday

English

1. c
2. b
3. d
4. answers will vary
5. 1d, 2c, 3a, 4b
6. island
7. share
8. d
9. a
10. right
11. weight
12. pear
13. come, close, do, slam, take
14. My parents read the Sunday papers out on the balcony.

Maths

1. 50, 66, 74, 88, 92, 101
2. 48, 58, 68, 78, 88, 90
3. 25, 50, 75, 100, 1, 99
4. 700
5. 152, 142, 132
6. 4 each
7. 10 cents
8. (a) 1:00   (b) 1:30
   (c) 1:05
9. 10 kg
10. (a) door   (b) truck
    (c) teacher (d) giraffe
    (e) elephant
11. c
12. c
13.
14. bases, square pyramid
15. parent/teacher check
16. parent/teacher check
17. 0

English

1. b
2. c
3. b
4. a wind
5. 1c, 2d, 3a, 4b
6. dried
7. plenty
8. d
9. b
10. shack
11. side
12. shot
13. jump, hop, bounce, pass, go
14. Uncle Bob took me to see the movie 'Back in Time'.

ANSWERS: *Excel* Basic Skills English and Mathematics Year 3

Answers

UNIT 18 page 50

Maths

1. 73, 93, 59, 65, 27, 31
2. 71, 63, 17, 47, 85, 89
3. 40, 100, 20, 60, 80, 30
4. 410
5. 296, 295, 294
6. 5 straws each with 1 left over
7. $2.60
8. (a) seven-thirty
   (b) half past seven
   (c) thirty minutes past seven
9. answers will vary
10. a
11. 12
12. 9 bottles
13. parent/teacher check
14. 8 straws
15. (a) zero   (b) one
16.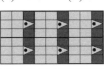
17.

boys	x	x	x	x				
girls	x	x	x	x	x	x	x	

English

1. c
2. a
3. c
4. Wayne Mitchell and A Mable
5. 1b, 2a, 3c, 4d
6. Doves
7. bread
8. d
9. b
10. fare
11. first
12. find
13. puppy, collar, leash, dish, toy, food, name
14. One night, I dreamt that I was Australia's Prime Minister.

UNIT 19 page 52

Maths

1. 45, 48, 46, 51, 44, 52
2. 60, 57, 62, 65, 56, 59
3. 8, 7, 4, 5, 10, 13
4. 111
5. 27, 31, 35, 39
6. 7 monkeys
7. 90 cents
8.
9. 10 bags
10. 3 pieces
11.
12. 3 L
13.
14. hexagonal prism
15.
16.
17. False

English

1. a
2. c
3. b
4. Beecroft
5. 1c, 2a, 3d, 4b
6. star
7. moon
8. b
9. c
10. This
11. Lost
12. spend
13. Flamingo, bird, ducks, geese, bird, metres, bill, feet
14. My band's name is 'Crazy Kids'.

UNIT 20 page 54

Maths

1. 24, 34, 44, 54, 64, 65
2. 16, 26, 36, 46, 56, 57
3. 20, 40, 60, 80, 100, 120
4. 653 ones
5. 8, 14, 16, 18, 24, 26, 32, 34, 36, 42, 44
6.
7. $1.90
8. (a) Tuesday   (b) May
9. food item
10. parent/teacher check
11. parent/teacher check
12. a fourth
13.
14.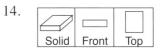

Solid	Front	Top

15. parallel lines
16.
17. (a) 2
    (b) 3

English

1. c
2. d
3. d
4. determined
5. 1c, 2d, 3a, 4b
6. sack
7. flood
8. c
9. c
10. Bridge
11. anybody
12. awoke
13. apple, hot, green, red
14. Mum said not to take Sharky to school because he bites.

Answers

UNIT 21 page 56

Maths

1. 22, 32, 42, 52, 62, 73
2. 85, 75, 65, 55, 45, 95
3. 1, 0, 2, 10, 3, 5
4. 700
5. forty cents, forty-five cents, fifty cents
6. (a) 4   (b) 5
   (c) 20   (d) 4, 5, 20
7. 50c + 20c + 20c + 5c
8. December, January, February
9. parent/teacher check
10. yes (5 cm)
11. a
12. 27 golf balls
13. cylinder
14. 1c, 2a, 3b
15. parent/teacher check
16.
17. parent/teacher check

English

1. d
2. b
3. c
4. the Thames
5. 1c, 2b, 3a, 4d
6. town
7. tear
8. d
9. b
10. Parking
11. pips
12. rang
13. they, me, I, I, them
14. I like having Katy and Chris over for dinner because Mum makes spaghetti bolognese.

UNIT 22 page 58

Maths

1. 66, 89, 97, 53, 58, 65
2. 5, 15, 25, 35, 45, 60
3. 7, 70, 0, 35, 84, 42
4. 31
5. (a) 41, 46, 51
   (b) 75, 72, 69
6. $7 \times 2 = 14$
7. 60c
8. (a) 25 December
   (b) May
9. food item
10. (a) 2 m 56 cm
    (b) 2 m 75 cm
    (c) 8 m 15 cm
11. 4 squares
12. B
13. (a)   (b)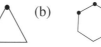

14. cone
15. a and d
16.
17. | x | x | x | | | |

English

1. c
2. b
3. d
4. answers will vary
5. 1c, 2a, 3b, 4d
6. church
7. bricks
8. b
9. c
10. feed
11. watch
12. Will
13. chocolate, caramel, favourite, orange
14. Every Saturday morning, I eat a bowl of Weetos with milk.

UNIT 23 page 60

Maths

1. 91, 18, 27, 52, 69, 74
2. 80, 70, 60, 50, 40, 90
3. 2, 10, 3, 9, 5, 8
4. 100
5. 426, 424, 422
6. 5, 10
7. 50c coin
8. (a) nine-oh-three
   (b) six-oh-five
9. about 24 small stones
10. (a) 1-chalk, 2-scissors, 3-table
    (b) 1-bike, 2-car, 3-truck
    (c) 1-toothpick, 2-pencil, 3-ruler
11. yes
12. 1 L
13. triangles, parallelogram, square
14.
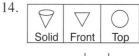		
Solid	Front	Top
15. 4 angles 
16. 10
17. 5

English

1. b
2. b
3. a
4. discarded
5. a, b
6. Beat
7. best
8. d
9. a
10. white
11. dish
12. deer
13. fish, busy, straw, fresh, new
14. Our school song is called 'Always do your best!'

Answers

ANSWERS: *Excel* Basic Skills English and Mathematics Year 3

Maths

1. 414, 424, 524, 624
2. (a) 5, 7, 2, 0, 4, 1, 6, 3, 19, 78
   (b) 5, 2, 10, 0, 7, 1, 6, 3, 89, 28
3. (a) 6, 18, 9, 24, 30, 12, 21, 15, 27
   and 12, 36, 18, 48, 60, 24,
   42, 30, 54
   (b) 45, 18, 63, 27, 72, 36, 81, 54,
   90 and 5, 2, 7, 3, 8, 4, 9, 6, 10
4. (a) 313
   (3 hundreds, 1 ten, 3 ones)
   (b) 129
   (1 hundred, 2 tens, 9 ones)
5. (a) 505, 506, 507, 508, 509
   (b) 400, 300, 200, 100, 0
   (c) 340, 350, 360, 370, 380, 390
   (d) 614, 612, 610, 608, 606, 604
6. (a) 6 pins   (b) 2 tomatoes
7. parent/teacher check
8. (a) 35   (b) 50
   (c) 30   (d) 5
9. 8 kg
10. (a) 100 cm (b) 500 cm
    (c) 900 cm
11. d
12. 6 glasses   13. square
14.
15. parent/teacher check
16. turn   17. 7

English

1. sausage rolls, mini pies,
   sandwich stacks, jam rolls,
   cupcakes, custard slices,
   ice-cream, strawberries,
   birthday cake
2. d   3. c
4. d   5. 1c, 2a, 3d, 4b
6. played   7. circle
8. a   9. d
10. eight   11. red
12. allowed
13. helped, decorate, cut, liked
14. (a) I invited ten friends to my
        party.
    (b) Have you seen Billy's gift?
    (c) Susan and Frank were
        invited too.

Maths

1. 64, 74, 84, 94, 104, 114
2. 0, 72, 792, 10, 180, 80
3. 50, 100, 150, 200, 250, 500
4. 98̲3
5. 991, 992, 993, 994, 995, 996,
   997
6. 6
7. 10 coins
8. Autumn
9. Elsa is heaviest by 3 kg
10. (a) 136 cm (b) 335 cm
11.
12. answers will vary
13. rhombus
14. parent/teacher check
15.
16.
17. 16

English

1. d
2. d
3. d
4. page 97
5. hinge, hippopotamus, hoarse,
   holiday
6. too
7. table
8. d
9. b
10. chess
11. log
12. past
13. Mary, stickers, pictures,
    bears, lions, dogs, album
14. I picked up my togs, cap,
    towel, powder and sunscreen
    and went to the pool.

Maths

1. 121, 123, 125, 127, 129, 128
2. 111, 110, 109, 108, 107, 112
3. 10, 20, 30, 40, 50, 55
4. c
5. 460, 470, 480, 490, 500, 510,
   520
6. 21 straws
7. (a) 1 dollar 65 cents
   (b) 0 dollars 80 cents
   (c) 145 cents
8. parent/teacher check
9. 4 packets
10. 1 m 15 cm
11. less than a square metre
12. parent/teacher check
13. (a) circular (b) triangular
    (c) rectangular
14. cube or square pyramid
15. parent/teacher check,
    4 angles
16.
17. 13

English

1. a
2. b
3. b
4. 45, 40, 35, 30, 25, 20
5. 1b, 2d, 3c, 4a
6. teeth
7. only
8. a
9. b
10. place
11. proud
12. pain
13. round, squeaky, slow, grey
14. Where are the next Olympic
    Games going to be held?

Answers

UNIT **26** page 70

Maths

1. 120, 130, 220, 230, 320, 400
2. 490, 390, 290, 190, 90, 100
3. 12, 24, 36, 48, 60, 120
4. 50 (5 tens)
5. 601, 501, 401, 301
6. 50, shade in 50 squares
7. no
8. two-oh-eight, eight minutes past two
   seven fifteen, fifteen minutes past seven
   four fifty-five, fifty-five minutes past four, or five minutes to five.
9. 12 kg
10. parent/teacher check
11. 16 squares
12. c
13. 80 m
14. vertex (point)
15.
16. b
17. 4

English

1. d
2. b
3. c
4. His dad invited him along.
5. 1c, 2b, 3a, 4d
6. lick
7. sheep
8. d
9. b
10. bent
11. gate
12. flu
13. use, cut, remember, throw, fold
14. Harold ran to the ticket office and then boarded the train.

UNIT **27** page 72

Maths

1. 40, 140, 240, 340, 440, 540
2. 0, 80, 60, 40, 20, 90
3. 1, 8, 6, 2, 5, 9
4. 880
5. 860, 880, 900, 920, 940, 960, 980
6. 10 hundredths
7. 15c, 10c, 10c, 65c
8. (a) 46   (b) 46
9. 4 tablespoons
10. 66 cm
11. parent/teacher check
12. tin of coffee
13.
14. 2
15. straight angle
16.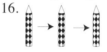
17. 10

English

1. c
2. d
3. d
4. a babysitter, a child's nurse
5. 1b, 2a, 3c, 4d
6. sight
7. Today
8. c
9. c or b
10. soon
11. marked
12. should, tied
13. was stung, hurt, cried, walked
14. Mount Cross Hospital is right next to Dollvale Shopping Centre.

UNIT **28** page 74

Maths

1. 100, 150, 200, 250, 300, 160
2. 0, 50, 100, 150, 200, 210
3. 15, 150, 300, 30, 3, 45
4. 919
5. 823, 822, 821, 820, 819, 818, 817
6. 53
7. 20 cent coin
8. Autumn
9. heavier
10. 125 cm
11. square
12. false
13.
14. sphere
15. sharp angle
16. many or endless or infinite
17. 10

English

1. c
2. c
3. a
4. about thirty kilograms
5. 1d, 2c, 3b, 4a
6. lunch
7. storm
8. a
9. d
10. tried
11. I'd
12. blast
13. Louisa, project, rocks, task, Thursday
14. I asked whether the treasure chest was for Peter or Paul.

Answers

UNIT 29 page 76

Maths

1. 302, 506, 618, 192, 787, 299
2. 750, 650, 550, 450, 350, 900
3. 200, 400, 600, 800, 1000, 300
4. 59
5. 499, 500, 501, 502, 503, 504, 505
6. 17
7. cross out 4 10c coins or 2 20c coins
8. (a) 53   (b) 7
   (c) 30
9. more than a kilogram
10. 2 m 53 cm
11. answers will vary
12. 50 L
13.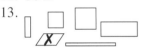
14. 6
15. blunt angle
16. Here

17. 5 cm

English

1. c
2. d
3. c
4. Grandma
5. 1c, 2d, 3a, 4b
6. down
7. dish
8. a
9. b
10. knead
11. toad
12. grey
13. she, it, her, she
14. 'Run, Nelly, Run', is a great book about a horse.

UNIT 30 page 78

Maths

1. 501, 510, 511, 600, 601, 900
2. 400, 420, 440, 460, 480, 499
3. 4, 10, 7, 8, 16, 20
4. 8
5. 724, 726, 728, 730, 732, 734, 736
6. 11, 1
7. $1.10 (110c)
8. (a) eleven forty-three
   (b) twelve fifty-seven
   (c) five twenty-eight
9. 14 kg
10. 120 cm
11. (a) 15   (b) 85
12. 10 L
13. parent/teacher check
14. (a) cube
    (b) rectangular prism
15.
16. a
17. Max

English

1. a
2. c
3. d
4. she had locked herself outside and the kettle was on
5. 1d, 2a, 3c, 4b
6. draw
7. dance
8. c
9. a
10. step
11. story
12. meet, knight
13. they, themselves, our, we, his
14. Do you know where you put my black boots?

TEST 4 page 80

Maths

1. 799 + 1 = 800 + 50 = 850 + 50 = 900 + 99 = 999
2. 70 runs
3. (a) 4   (b) 8
   (c) 6   (d) 5 r 2
4. (a) 463   (b) 982
   (c) 756   (d) 500
5. (a) 727, 730, 733, 736, 739
   (b) 602, 612, 622, 632, 642
6. (a) 100   (b) 30 hundredths
   (c) 70 hundredths
   (d) 10 hundredths
7. 7 more coins
8. (a)   (b)
9. 12 packets
10. circled: gum tree, across the room, a path, a truck, a bed, beach umbrella, a street
    ticked: your arm, ruler, cat
11. 9 times
12. green: milk, lunch box, salad oil.
    blue: cream, medicine glass, cola, jam, mug, shampoo.
    yellow: chlorine, apple juice, oil, orange juice.
13. triangle, 3, 3   square, 4, 4 pentagon, 5, 5 hexagon, 6, 6 octagon, 8, 8
14. square pyramid
15. Z   16.
17. 11

English

1. c   2. c   3. d
4. answers will vary
5. 1c, 2a, 3d, 4b   6. handle
7. Tennis   8. a
9. d   10. wear
11. steel   12. soles
13. Tennis, sport, people, player, racquet, handle, leather
14. Tennis racquets are made out of wood, steel, graphite or aluminium.

Mathematics

Measurement and Geometry

8. Write in digital form the time shown on each clock.

(a)   (b)   (c)   (d)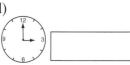

9. Mum bought a kilogram of bananas and two kilograms of oranges. I then bought a kilogram of apples. How many kilograms of fruit did we buy altogether?

10. Is each more than a metre, about a metre or less than a metre?

(a) height of a door ☐ (b) width of a door ☐ (c) a book ☐ (d) a boot ☐

11. How many blocks have been used to build this model?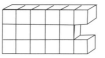

12. How many blocks are there in each model?

(a)   (b)   (c)   (d)

13. Which of these statements about rectangles is not true?
(a) Rectangles are very thin. (b) The long side of the rectangle is the length.
(c) All rectangles have a breadth.

14. Name each of these solid shapes. The names are listed in the box.

cone	cube
sphere	cylinder
pyramid	
rectangular prism	

15. Which angle is a right angle?

16. Which pictures **flip**, **slide** or **turn**? (a)   (b)   (c)
(a)
(b)
(c)

Statistics and Probability

17. Which food was eaten the most?
pizza ⵌ ⵌ || chips ⵌ ⵌ ⵌ ⵌ
chicken ⵌ ⵌ   hamburgers |||

RESCUE FROM HILLSIDE FIRE

Boys haul pal from pit ...

Two young boys yesterday afternoon dragged their 10-year-old mate to safety from a blazing four-metre-deep pit.

The boy, Errol Anseley, of Cheviot Street, Upper Frenchs Forest, escaped with slight burns to his right leg and arm. His mates helped him to safety before the flames could catch his clothes.

The boys were using the mountainside pit in Upper Mt Gravatt as a cubbyhouse. They lit a small campfire in the pit, which Errol looked after while the others went for more firewood.

Bushfire begins ...

The two boys dropped some dry weeds down the hole but they fell onto the fire which then blazed up. The flames spread to the edge of the pit and started a bushfire which was still burning last night.

Errol's mates helped him home and an ambulance took him to the Mater Childrens' Hospital for observation. His condition is satisfactory.

Reading and Comprehension

1. Where were the boys while Errol was in the pit?
   (a) They were bushwalking.
   (b) They hadn't arrived yet.
   (c) They were collecting firewood.
   (d) They were ringing the ambulance.

2. How did the fire start in the first place?
   (a) A bushfire began nearby.
   (b) The boys were smoking.
   (c) The clothes were on fire.
   (d) The boys lit a small campfire.

3. In which suburb did this incident happen?
   (a) Brisbane
   (b) Frenchs Forest
   (c) Upper Mt Gravatt
   (d) Mater Hill

4. Find another word which means 'friend'.

   _____

   _____

5. Number these sentences in order (1–4).
   (a) Errol guarded the pit.
   (b) The bushfire began to spread.
   (c) The boys found a cubbyhouse.
   (d) They lit a small campfire.

Spelling and Vocabulary

Rewrite the misspelt words.

6. His mates helpt him to get out of the pit.

   _____

   _____

   _____

7. Their tin year old friend was in trouble.

   _____

   _____

   _____

Circle the correct word in brackets.

8. The boys dropped the (would, wood) down the hole.

9. (There, Their) friend was dragged to safety.

10. Cross out the word which is different.
    (a) pit, deep, ditch, hole
    (b) friend, pal, boy, mate
    (c) little, him, young, small

Circle the word from the list that has the nearest meaning to the underlined word.

11. His condition is <u>satisfactory</u>.
    (a) excellent
    (b) unwell
    (c) alright
    (d) poorly

12. He escaped with <u>slight</u> burns.
    (a) minor
    (b) dreadful
    (c) painful
    (d) small

Grammar and Punctuation

13. Underline the **nouns** in these sentences.

    Errol is a lucky boy. His pals saved him. An ambulance took him to the hospital for an examination.

14. Punctuate and capitalise this sentence.

    errol anseley is from frenchs forest and he was hauled from a four-metre pit

    _____

    _____

    _____

    _____

Mathematics

Number and Algebra

1.

+	50	62	78	53	89	99
1						

2.

–	90	57	88	43	70	71
1						

3.

×	24	68	38	43	77	99
1						

4. Write the numeral made up of three hundreds, six tens and four ones.

5. 154, 164, 174, ☐ , ☐ , ☐

6.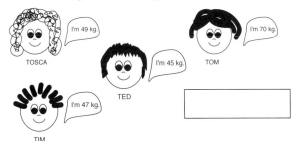

☐ groups of ☐ bats

7. 3 lots of 50c = ☐

Measurement and Geometry

8. Today is Tuesday. What day of the week was it one week ago?

9. Who weighs two kilograms more than Ted?

TOSCA — I'm 49 kg.
TOM — I'm 70 kg.
TED — I'm 45 kg.
TIM — I'm 47 kg.

10. Match each task with its correct distance.
Rule a line • 10 m
Jumping race • 10 cm
Throw a ball • 100 m

11. How many squares of this number puzzle are for writing answers in?

☐

12. How many litres are in the tank?

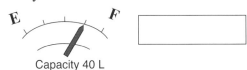

Capacity 40 L

☐

13. Draw the next plane shape in this pattern.

14. Which shape is different? Why?

A   B   C   D

15. Show 3 o'clock on this clock. What sort of angle have you made?

☐

16. Which square has the greater number of lines of symmetry — A or B?

A   B   ☐

Statistics and Probability

17. On which day were the most snails sighted? ☐

Weekdays	Snails Sighted
Sunday	🐌 🐌
Monday	
Tuesday	🐌 🐌 🐌 🐌
Wednesday	
Thursday	🐌
Friday	🐌
Saturday	🐌 🐌 🐌

Our best mission

We had been circling Planet X for some time now. Our spaceship was in good hands. Captain Minas knew how to control the spacecraft for he was the best astronaut Australia had.

The view from our spaceship window was just breathtaking. It was so dark and calm. All we could see were lots of large dots. Some dots were faraway planets and some of them were stars. Planet X was our destination.

I had my own job to do; ten, nine, eight, seven, six … this was the moment for which I had trained. As a young boy I had always wanted to be an astronaut and now my dream was about to come true.

Five, four, three, two, one … THUMP! We had landed the Spaceship Koalan. Captain Minas and I checked our spacesuits and made sure they were well fitted. I had my space camera around my neck and Captain Minas was prepared to collect the rock samples.

We could see astronaut Thomas through our visors and he waved at us as we planted the Australian flag into Planet X's surface. I jumped for joy and luckily I had my space boots on!

Reading and Comprehension

1. The spaceship was in good hands because
(a) it was the Koalan.
(b) it was new and strong.
(c) Captain Minas was on board.
(d) I had trained to be an astronaut.

2. How many astronauts were there altogether?
(a) 4 (b) 3
(c) 2 (d) 1

3. Which item was not worn by the astronauts?
(a) camera
(b) space suits
(c) space boots
(d) flag

4. Think of your own reason why the space boots were so important.

_____

_____

5. Number these sentences in order (1–4).
(a) We opened Koalan's hatch.
(b) We could see astronaut Thomas.
(c) We landed on Planet X.
(d) The view was beautiful.

Spelling and Vocabulary

Rewrite the misspelt words.

6. Australia is the only iland continent of the world. _____

7. Please shair the jelly beans with Mary. _____

Circle the word that has the nearest meaning to the underlined word.

8. I don't wish to <u>alarm</u> you but there is a spider on your leg.
(a) ring (b) help
(c) tell (d) frighten

9. She <u>blamed</u> her baby sister for the messy room.
(a) accused
(b) banged
(c) brought
(d) patted

Circle the correct word in brackets.

10. The bus turned (right, write) at the next intersection.

11. Step on the scales and find out your (weight, wait).

12. The (pear, pair) was badly bruised.

Grammar and Punctuation

13. Underline the **verbs** in these sentences.

Come here. Close the door behind you. Please do not slam it. Now, take a seat!

14. Punctuate and capitalise this sentence.

my parents read the sunday papers out on the balcony

_____

_____

Number and Algebra

1.

+	48	64	72	86	90	99
2						

2.

−	50	60	70	80	90	92
2						

3.

÷	25	50	75	100	1	99
1						

4. Write the numeral for seven hundred.

5. 182, 172, 162, ☐ , ☐ , ☐

6. Share sixteen pencils among 4 children.

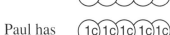

7. Emma has

Paul has

How many cents are there altogether?

Measurement and Geometry

8. Show on the digital clocks:
(a) 1 o'clock (b) half past one (c) '1-oh-5'

☐ : ☐   ☐ : ☐   ☐ : ☐

9. What is the total mass of 5 bags of rice?

RICE 2 kg

10. Which is longer than one metre:
(a) your pencil or the classroom door?
(b) a truck or this book?
(c) a baby or your teacher?
(d) a giraffe or a kitten?
(e) a dolly or an elephant?

11. Circle the shape that would tessellate.
(a)   (b)   (c)

12. Each fuel tank holds 40 L. Which one shows 10 L? ☐
(a)   (b)   (c)

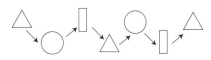

13. Draw the next two shapes in the pattern.

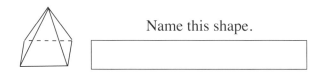

14. Prisms and pyramids are named according to the shape of their b __ __ __ __ .

Name this shape.

15. On this dot paper draw a right angle.

· · · · · ·
· · · · · ·
· · · · · ·
· · · · · ·
· · · · · ·

16. Draw in the mirror image.

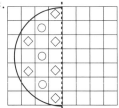

Statistics and Probability

17.

Blue eyes	😀 👧 🙂 👦 🙂
Brown eyes	

How many children have brown eyes? ☐

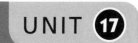
The dove and the ant

One day an ant was crawling along very quickly on its six legs, when suddenly it stopped on a creek bank.

"Mmm … I feel a bit thirsty," said the tiny ant out aloud.

A dove that was perched on a tree branch nearby overheard the ant and said, "Take a drink from the creek if you like. Enjoy your drink but be careful not to fall in little friend." The ant sped off down the bank but suddenly, a wind blew him into the water. "I'm drowning!" cried the helpless ant. "Help me! Somebody help me!"

Luckily, the dove was close by. With its sharp beak, the dove broke off a twig from the tree and dropped it beside the ant. Ant climbed onto the twig and floated safely to shore.

The next day, the ant noticed a hunter in the woods. He was bird shooting and had his eye on the dove. Ant had to think quickly! I have to help my friend, he thought. The ant opened his strong jaws and gave the hunter a big bite on the ankle.

"Ouch … that hurt!" cried the hunter. The dove saw the hunter and waved to his little friend, then flew away.

Moral: one good turn deserves another.

Reading and Comprehension

1. Why did the ant go to the creek edge in the first place?
    (a) He saw the dove.
    (b) He was thirsty.
    (c) His ant friend was in trouble.
    (d) He found a twig.

2. Dove saved ant by throwing him a
    (a) branch.   (b) leaf.
    (c) twig.   (d) tree.

3. Ant bit the hunter on the ankle because
    (a) his jaws were strong.
    (b) he was going to shoot dove.
    (c) one good turn deserves another.
    (d) ant knows how to act quickly.

4. What caused ant to topple into the water?

    _____

5. Number these sentences in order (1–4).
    (a) Dove threw a twig.
    (b) Ant floated ashore.
    (c) Ant was thirsty.
    (d) He fell in the creek.

Spelling and Vocabulary

Rewrite the misspelt words.

6. Mum dried the plants
    by using her flower press. _____

7. You can buy plentea of
    stone fruit during summer. _____

Circle the word that has the nearest meaning to the underlined word.

8. This cement <u>path</u> leads to Lee's house.
    (a) street   (b) park
    (c) block   (d) slab

9. The science project was <u>done</u> by Friday.
    (a) drawn   (b) completed
    (c) rushed   (d) collected

Circle the correct word in brackets.

10. The (shake, shack) is the only one left from the early pioneer days.

11. Which soccer (side, slide) are you in?

12. She aimed the (shot, shoot) and won herself a blue teddybear.

Grammar and Punctuation

13. Underline the **verbs** in these sentences.

    Jump to the left and hop to the right. Bounce six times before you pass the beanbag. Go now!

14. Punctuate and capitalise this sentence.

    uncle bob took me to see the movie back in time

    _____

    _____

Number and Algebra

1.

+	71	91	57	63	25	29
2						

2.

–	73	65	19	49	87	91
2						

3.

×	20	50	10	30	40	15
2						

4. Write the numeral for:

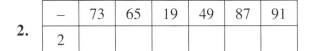

5. 299, 298, 297, ⬚ , ⬚ , ⬚

6. Share 16 straws among 3 children. How many straws are left over?

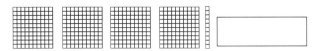

7. I have a $2 coin and three 20c coins. How much do I have to spend?

Measurement and Geometry

8. Show three different ways to say this time.   7 : 30

  1.
  2.
  3.

9. Which one 'feels' heavier— your shoe or your pencil case?

10. Which one is the best measure for the height of the teacher's desk?
  (a) 1 metre   (b) 100 mm   (c) 10 cm

11. Prunella put a sheet of clear plastic over this tiled pattern. How many whole tiles does it cover?

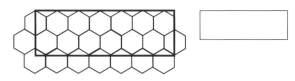

12. How many bottles of oil do I need to make 9 L?

13. Colour all the lines going up and down green.

14. How many straws have been used to make this skeleton model?

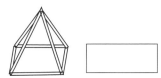

15. At how many points does each group of lines cross?

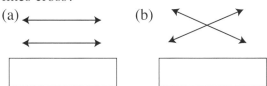

(a)   (b)

16. Complete these tiles by **sliding** to the right.

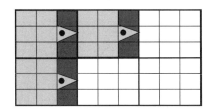

Statistics and Probability

17. Use the boxes to compare the 2 groups.

4 boys						

7 girls						

Just give me a call!

Read this information out loud and answer the questions.

M	Mable	894
Mable A 16 Tulip St Greenwood		362 2048
Mable T 118 Rose St Home Creek		384 7085
Mason MJ 74 Hill Rd The Grove		391 6759
Mason Peter 20 North Rd Bat Point		382 0099
Michael A 10 Sing St Ball Park		343 1213
Michael's Chemist 602 Bells Rd Berrydale		372 2211
Michaels Tom Lucky Rd Rivertown		359 4570
Mitchell Lyn 100 Swan St Lolo		389 3971
Mitchell M 111 Lucky Ave Northtown		329 1284
Mitchell VK 84 Paint St Yenton		364 0980
Mitchell Wayne 19 Queen Ave Greenwood		368 1185
Mople D 200 Summer St Westcook		324 0004
Morton C&K 189 Booking Tce Greenbank		302 9994
Morton's Electrical 2 Club Rd Taradale		300 2626
Morton's Swimming School		
18 Waterloo Rd Fish Bay		308 4622
Moss B 134 Butter St Honeydale		319 2258
Moss X&R 19 Dingo Dr Turry		328 8999
Moss Zoe 123 Rolling Rd Kotton		348 1116
Mossle C 456 Cuptown St South End		306 5555
Mother Hubbard's Bookstore		
101 Bone Rd Dogtown		384 0123
Mt Grass Markets		
Third Avenue Mowingvale		386 1997

Reading and Comprehension

1. What is Lyn Mitchell's phone number?
    (a) 328 8999
    (b) 364 0980
    (c) 389 3971
    (d) 362 2048

2. What is the address of the Swimming School?
    (a) 18 Waterloo Rd
    (b) 101 Bone Rd
    (c) 84 Paint St
    (d) 74 Hill Rd

3. In what suburb is Zoe Moss living?
    (a) Lolo   (b) Berrydale
    (c) Kotton   (d) The Grove

4. Two people listed live in the same suburb. Who are they?

    _____

5. Number these surnames in order (1–4).
    (a) Michael   (b) Mable
    (c) Mople   (d) Moss

Spelling and Vocabulary

Rewrite the misspelt words.

6. Duvs are small birds which belong in the family of pigeons.

    _____

7. My favourite bred is multigrain.

    _____

Circle the word that has the nearest meaning to the underlined word.

8. <u>Clean</u> this woolly jumper in warm water.
    (a) polish   (b) dye   (c) dry   (d) wash

9. The <u>chair</u> I sat on had chewing gum on it.
    (a) cushion   (b) seat
    (c) beanbag   (d) furniture

Circle the correct word in brackets.

10. Bill had a five-dollar note to pay his bus (fare, fair).

11. Sharon came (fist, first) and I came second.

12. Dad couldn't (fine, find) his blue jeans.

Grammar and Punctuation

13. Underline the **nouns** in these sentences.

    Before you buy a puppy, make sure you've bought a collar, leash, dish, toy and some food. Think of a name for it.

14. Punctuate and capitalise this sentence.

    one night i dreamt that i was australia's prime minister

    _____

    _____

Number and Algebra

1.

+	42	45	43	48	41	49
3						

2.

–	63	60	65	68	59	62
3						

3.

÷	16	14	8	10	20	26
2						

4. Write the numeral which is made up of one hundred and eleven ones.

5. Complete this (+4) number pattern.

15, 19, 23, [ ], [ ], [ ], [ ]

6. How many monkeys could be given 2 bananas each?

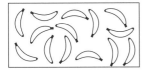

7. Dad gave me 10 cents for every spelling word I got right. If I received 9 out of 10 for spelling, how much did Dad owe me?

Measurement and Geometry

8.  20 minutes later

9. How many bags of flour would it take to make 10 kg?

1 kg   FLOUR

10. How many 2 cm pieces of rope could I make out of this long piece?

11. Tesselate this shape six times.

12. Miriam found that it took 12 eggcups to fill a 1 L jug with water. How many litres did she use if she filled 36 eggcups?

13. Cross out the shape that doesn't belong.

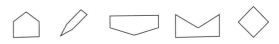

14. Circle the right name for this 3D shape.

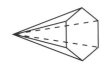

pentagonal prism
hexagonal prism

15. Draw any 3 lines that cross at the same point.

16. Draw in the lines of symmetry.

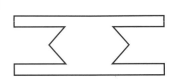

Statistics and Probability

17.

Mon	Tues	Wed	Thu	Fri	Sat	Sun
☀	☀	☁	☁	🌧		🌧

It was cloudy on Friday.

☐ True   ☐ False

5 Forest Way, Beecroft
Sunday 2/3/12

Dear Joel,

Just a short letter to tell you we got here OK. Thanks for seeing us off. Wow, this is an upside-down place! I guess that's why they call it downunder. You know how cold it was in Madison and Chicago when we left, snow on the ground and all. Well, it was RED HOT when we landed. I was boiling in my jacket. I sure took it off fast. And you know what? They drive cars on the wrong side of the road. It's a ~~wunder~~ wonder there aren't more accidents.

I couldn't understand the cab driver at first. Aussies sure speak with funny voices. He kept saying "You'll loik it here mite." He meant "You'll LIKE it here MATE" (I think). They call everyone "mite" (mate). It means "buddy". But why don't they say so?

Our house has no basement. Wonder where I'll play when it snows. Oops, There's no snow in ~~Sidney~~ Sydney. Wouldn't you bet? It's not a bad house though. Some great trees to climb in the garden. They call them gum trees, the taxi driver said. Bet you'd be in ~~truble~~ trouble if you tried to chew the gum from them. It would stick your teeth together.

I'll write next week.

Stevie

From *Stevie Comes to Stay* by Gordon Winch

Reading and Comprehension

1. On what side of the road do cars in Chicago drive?
    (a) right   (b) left
    (c) drive   (d) wrong

2. The American term for *mate* is
    (a) friend.   (b) mite.
    (c) buddy.   (d) Mike.

3. Stevie wrote this letter
    (a) in Madison.
    (b) on Sunday.
    (c) while he chewed gum.
    (d) when it was RED HOT!

4. In what suburb is Stevie living now?

    _____

5. Number these sentences in order (1–4).
    (a) Stevie took off his jacket.
    (b) There was no snow.
    (c) Joel saw Stevie off.
    (d) He couldn't understand the cab driver.

Spelling and Vocabulary

Rewrite the misspelt words.

6. The largest sdar in our
    solar system is the Sun. _____

7. Man first walked
    on the moun in 1969. _____

Circle the word that has the nearest meaning to the underlined word.

8. The clowns stood in the middle of the <u>ring</u>.
    (a) diamond   (b) circle
    (c) oval   (d) shape

9. The <u>clothes</u> he wore were made out of cotton.
    (a) jeans   (b) jersey
    (c) garments   (d) pyjamas

Circle the correct word in brackets.

10. (This, These) boy is new at our school.

11. He returned the hat to (Lost, Last) Property.

12. I asked Mum if I could (spent, spend) ten dollars.

Grammar and Punctuation

13. Underline the **nouns** in these sentences.

    The flamingo is a water bird which is related to ducks and geese. This bird can grow to 1.5 metres from the bill to the feet.

14. Punctuate and capitalise this sentence.

    my band's name is crazy kids

    _____

    _____

Number and Algebra

1.

+	20	30	40	50	60	61
4						

2.

−	20	30	40	50	60	61
4						

3.

×	5	10	15	20	25	30
4						

4. How many ones make up this total number: 653?

5. Write in the missing numbers:

2, 4, 6, ___ , 10, 12, ___ , ___ ,

___ , 20, 22, ___ , ___ , 28, 30,

___ , ___ , ___ , 38, 40,

___ , ___

6. Make 2 shares.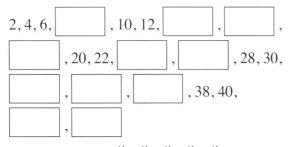

7.

TUCKSHOP MENU

Meat pie	80c	Orange juice	$1
Sausage roll	90c	Milk drink	$1
Salad roll	75c	Cup of soup	50c

I ordered a milk drink and a sausage roll. How much money did I spend?

Measurement and Geometry

8. (a) I am the day after Monday.

(b) I am the month before June.

9. Which is heavier—the mass or the food item?

10. This fish is 2 cm. Draw one twice as long.

11. Colour the largest shape red and the smallest shape green.

12. Seeto used 1 L of soft drink to equally fill four glasses. What part of a litre did each glass hold?

13. Use three lines to make this shape into 1 square and 3 triangles.

14. Complete this table.

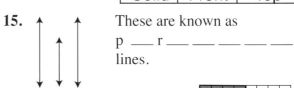

Solid	Front	Top

15. These are known as p ___ r ___ ___ ___ ___ ___ lines.

16. Complete this tile pattern by sliding the tiles four squares to the right.

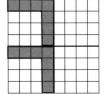

Statistics and Probability

17. (a) How many shoelaces are long?

(b) How many more short shoelaces are there than long shoelaces?

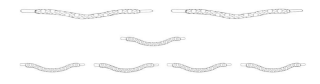

Kylie the kangaroo

Kylie was a small kangaroo. She was small when she was a joey in her mother's pouch and she was small when she grew up. No matter how much Kylie ate, she didn't seem to grow any bigger. She was small when she started and she stayed small.

Being small was a big problem for Kylie. The other kangaroos laughed at her when they all went walking, because Kylie couldn't keep up.

All kangaroos went walking in those days, for the simple reason that they had not heard of hopping. A small kangaroo like Kylie took very tiny steps and she was always left behind in the hot Australian sun. Kylie came last in the Kangaroo Carnival Races and she felt really bad about it. Then she was knocked out in the first round of the Kangaroo Boxing Tournament. Kylie felt bad about that too. When all the kangaroos went to watch the tennis, little Kylie could not even see. She felt even worse.

But in spite of it all, Kylie kept trying. She was small and she was sad, but she was also very determined. Kylie never gave up. She entered all the races and all the boxing tournaments. And she always went walking with the other kangaroos, even though she was always left behind.

From Kylie the Kangaroo by Gordon Winch

Reading and Comprehension

1. What was Kylie's big problem?
   (a) She was a kangaroo.
   (b) She came last on Carnival Day.
   (c) She was small in size.
   (d) She couldn't watch the tennis game.

2. A joey is
   (a) an enormous animal.
   (b) a mother kangaroo's pouch.
   (c) the name of a tournament.
   (d) a baby kangaroo.

3. Why did the kangaroos go walking?
   (a) They were too young to hop.
   (b) They were tired.
   (c) They lived close by.
   (d) They had not heard of hopping.

4. Complete this sentence.
   Kylie the kangaroo was very

   ___ et ___ ___ ___ ___ ___ ___ d.

5. Number these sentences in order (1–4).
   (a) She came last in the races.
   (b) She kept on trying.
   (c) Kylie was a small kangaroo.
   (d) She took very tiny steps.

Spelling and Vocabulary

Rewrite the misspelt words.

6. Mrs Claus put a few toys in the sac.

   _____

7. The flud destroyed the carpets in our house.

   _____

Circle the word that has the nearest meaning to the underlined word.

8. Mum had to read a <u>book</u> on 'Driving Rules'.
   (a) notebook   (b) puzzle
   (c) manual   (d) paper

9. Dad tried to <u>kick</u> his smoking habit.
   (a) shoot   (b) goal
   (c) stop   (d) keep

Circle the correct word in brackets.

10. Where is the Golden Gate (Brige, Bridge)?

11. Does (anybody, anybodie) have a pencil?

12. The bear (woke, awoke) after a deep winter's sleep.

Grammar and Punctuation

13. Underline the **adjectives** in these sentences.

    The apple cake was in the hot oven. Mum made the green icing. She cut the red cherries.

14. Punctuate and capitalise this sentence.

    mum said not to take sharky to school because he bites

    _____

    _____

Number and Algebra

1.

+	17	27	37	47	57	68
5						

2.

–	90	80	70	60	50	100
5						

3.

÷	9	0	18	90	27	45
9						

4. What is the value of the digit in bold—**7**28?

5. Complete the pattern:
twenty cents, twenty-five cents, thirty cents,

thirty-five cents, _____ ,

_____ ,

_____

6. ○○○○○   (a) How many rows are there?
○○○○○
○○○○○
○○○○○   (b) How many are there in each row?

(c) Estimate and count the

number altogether. _____

(d) ____ groups of ____ = ____

7. Show 95 cents using four coins only.

Measurement and Geometry

8. What are the 3 summer months?

1. _____

2. _____

3. _____

9. Find three different packages in the kitchen that hold 2 kg.

1. _____

2. _____

3. _____

10. Are these lines equal? Measure them to find out their length.

11. Elmo found out how many 20c coins could fit the length of his ruler. Circle the correct one.

(a) 11 coins   (b) 3 coins   (c) 30 coins

12. Fred could fit 9 golf balls in a box. How many golf balls could he put in 3 boxes?

13. From which solid shape can you make these plane shapes?

14. Match the information with the right solid name.

1. pyramid   (a) 6 squares
2. cube   (b) 6 rectangles
3. rectangular prism   (c) 4 triangles, 1 square

15. Explain how you would make a right angle out of a piece of paper.

16. Prove that a rectangle tesselates.

Statistics and Probability

17. Draw rows of pictures to represent how many pencils and erasers are in your pencil case.

✏	
▱	

Why did Europeans settle in Australia?

The first Europeans to settle in Australia were known as convicts. A convict was a person who was found guilty of a crime and was sent to prison. Back in Britain, many, many years ago, the jails became very overcrowded. Something had to be done.

The British used old ships known as hulks as extra jails. These hulks were tied up in British rivers like the Thames. The hulks became smelly and diseases broke out, and the convicts tried to escape.

British cities grew and grew. More and more people were working in factories, mines and on farms. New machinery meant less workers were needed and, before long, jobs were hard to find. Some people just could not get work! Working long hours, people still received very poor pay. Women and children had to work too. These poor conditions led more people to crime.

The British Government had to think of an answer. If convicts were sent away, they would have little chance of escaping the hulks. They could be made to develop new lands by farming, making buildings and roads. It made more sense than using the old ships as prison houses.

It took about seven months to get to Botany Bay …

Reading and Comprehension

1. A convict was a person who
   (a) lived on a hulk.
   (b) worked in a factory.
   (c) couldn't find work.
   (d) was found guilty of a crime.

2. Old ships used as jails were called
   (a) jail houses.   (b) hulks.
   (c) prisoners.   (d) prisons.

3. How long did the voyage to Australia take?
   (a) seven weeks   (b) seven days
   (c) seven months   (d) seven years

4. What is the river named in the passage?

   _____

5. Number these sentences in order (1–4).
   (a) British cities grew and grew.
   (b) Hulks were used as jails.
   (c) Crime was a real problem.
   (d) The voyage took seven months.

Spelling and Vocabulary

Rewrite the misspelt words.

6. Another word for toun is city. _____

7. Emily had a teer in her eye. _____

Circle the word that has the nearest meaning to the underlined word.

8. Put your money in a safe place for now.
   (a) locked   (b) bank
   (c) purse   (d) secure

9. If you get there early, keep a seat for me.
   (a) kick   (b) reserve
   (c) catch   (d) buy

Circle the correct word in brackets.

10. (Parking, Park) in this spot is prohibited.

11. A mandarin can have over fifty (pips, pipes).

12. The bell (rung, rang) and the students moved.

Grammar and Punctuation

13. Underline the **pronouns** in these sentences.

    The twins sat in a circle. They moved beside me. I was in the middle. I liked them.

14. Punctuate and capitalise this sentence.

    i like having katy and chris over for dinner because mum makes spaghetti bolognese

    _____

    _____

Number and Algebra

1.

+	60	83	91	47	52	59
6						

2.

–	11	21	31	41	51	66
6						

3.

×	1	10	0	5	12	6
7						

4. Write the numeral for:

5. (a) 21, 26, 31, 36, ☐ , ☐ , ☐

   (b) 87, 84, 81, 78, ☐ , ☐ , ☐

6. 7 lots of

   ☐ × ☐ = ☐

7. Christina borrowed $1.20 from Sammy. She has only paid back half of it. How much does she still owe?

   20c 20c 20c 20c 20c 20c ☐

Measurement and Geometry

8. (a) What is the date of Christmas Day? ☐

   (b) What is the fifth month of the year? ☐

9. Which is lighter—the mass or the food item?

   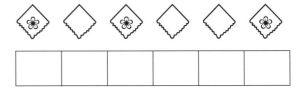 ☐

10. Complete:

    (a) 256 cm = ☐ m ☐ cm

    (b) 275 cm = ☐ m ☐ cm

    (c) 815 cm = ☐ m ☐ cm

11. How many squares fill this area? 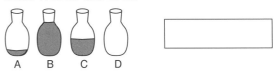 ☐

12. A vinegar bottle holds one litre. Which one is it?

    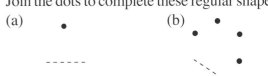
    A B C D   ☐

13. Join the dots to complete these regular shapes.

    (a)   (b)

    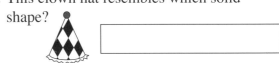

14. This clown hat resembles which solid shape?

    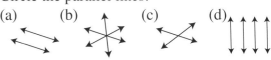 ☐

15. Circle the parallel lines.

    (a)   (b)   (c)   (d)

16. Draw the swan's **reflection**.

Statistics and Probability

17. In these squares draw one cross to represent each handkerchief with a flower on it.

My grandad George

My grandad George was born a very long time ago. He is now sixty-seven years old and I try to visit him as much as I can. I'm not really interested in writing but I love to talk about him. He has so much to tell me about his childhood and life. By now, I probably know more about him than my parents do.

He doesn't like sports and he hates watching videos. You'll never find him near a shopping centre either. I know that he enjoys working in his garden. He has grown spinach, beans and tomatoes. I often help him with the weeding and watering.

Grandad George has always had grey hair. Well, to my knowledge anyway. His front teeth are stained from smoking too much. It upsets me that he smokes a lot and that he doesn't look after his health.

He was born in a village in Greece. His village is high on the hillside. I've never been there but he tells me it's famous for growing olives and figs. During the Second World War, he says, food was scarce. He said he had his own farmlet to look after and that meat and bread were very dear.

Grandad had to get water from a well and he used an old tin to scoop it up. He said that his parents made extra money selling kerosene tins and oil lanterns. He often tells me how homesick he is. I'd like to go to Europe one day.

Reading and Comprehension

1. What relation is the child to grandad George?
   (a) son   (b) daughter
   (c) grandchild   (d) nephew

2. What bad habit does grandad have?
   (a) shopping   (b) smoking
   (c) greying   (d) talking

3. During the Second World War, what was expensive?
   (a) olives   (b) kerosene tins
   (c) cigarettes   (d) meat

4. In a few words, tell why your grandparents are so special.

   _____

   _____

5. Number these sentences in order (1–4).
   (a) He doesn't like shopping.
   (b) He was born in a Greek village.
   (c) I visit Grandad a lot.
   (d) It's on a hillside.

Spelling and Vocabulary

Rewrite the misspelt words.

6. The pews at our churtch are from America.

   _____

7. Some briks are dried in the sun.

   _____

Circle the word that has the nearest meaning to the underlined word.

8. The police <u>chased</u> the man who was speeding.
   (a) caught   (b) followed
   (c) saw   (d) knew

9. We took the lift to the <u>ground</u> floor.
   (a) gravel   (b) top
   (c) bottom   (d) grassy

Circle the correct word in brackets.

10. Only (fed, feed) the fish a tiny amount of food.

11. My (wash, watch) needs a new battery.

12. (We'll, Will) Tabatha know about it?

Grammar and Punctuation

13. Underline the **adjectives** in these sentences.

    I like chocolate shakes and caramel toffees.
    My favourite lollies are those orange buttons.

14. Punctuate and capitalise this sentence.

    every saturday morning i eat a bowl of weetos with milk

    _____

    _____

    _____

Mathematics

Number and Algebra

1.

+	84	11	20	45	62	67
7						

2.

−	87	77	67	57	47	97
7						

3.

÷	16	80	24	72	40	64
8						

4. Write the numeral for:

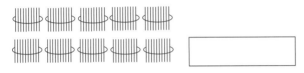

5. 432, 430, 428, ____, ____, ____

6.

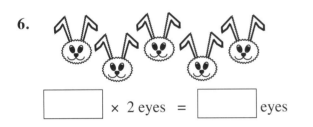

☐ × 2 eyes = ☐ eyes

7. I am the largest silver coin with twelve straight edges. I have a kangaroo and an emu on one side. Which coin am I? ☐

Measurement and Geometry

8. Complete the labels.

(a) **9 : 03** (b) **6 : 05**

nine-oh-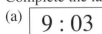 -oh-five

9. A bottle has the same mass as a dozen small stones. Two bottles have the same mass as ☐ small stones.

10. Number each group (1– 3) from shortest to longest.

(a) chalk, table, scissors.

(b) truck, bike, car.

(c) pencil, toothpick, ruler.

11. Does this shape tessellate—yes or no?

12. 2 × half a litre = ☐

13. Which plane shapes have been used to make this 'person' picture.

14. Complete this table:

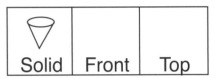

Solid	Front	Top

15. How many angles can you find in the letter H? Colour them in red. ☐

16. Guess how many lines of symmmetry a regular 10-sided shape has. ☐

Statistics and Probability

17. What is the difference between the shoes and the socks? ☐

60

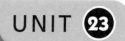

Recycling

Australians are smart people. We like to recycle. We can help the environment by recycling because it saves a lot of the Earth's natural resources. All it means is that you take old discarded materials and make new items (products) from them.

Lots of materials can be recycled. Aluminium cans, cardboard, glass, paper and plastic bottles can be recycled to make new products. In Australia, most household waste is buried. Old sites are rapidly filling and it is becoming harder to find new sites. We can reduce our disposal problem by reducing our waste. How can we do that? We can reuse waste items whenever possible or recycle waste items to use the raw (base) material again.

Did you know that Australia has one of the best aluminium-can recycling programs in the world? Old aluminium cans can be turned back into new aluminium cans. This reduces the amount of waste going into landfill. Once again, this is good for the Australian environment.

You can also be paid extra cash for collecting aluminium cans and this helps keep the grounds clean too. Recycling produces jobs and recycled aluminium can be exported which is good for the Australian economy.

Reading and Comprehension

1. Australians are smart people because they like to
   (a) produce.   (b) recycle.
   (c) clean.   (d) waste.

2. Recycling old used products results in
   (a) buying more items.
   (b) saving natural resources.
   (c) discarding used items.
   (d) finding new landfill areas.

3. The main benefit of recycling aluminium cans is
   (a) it can keep the environment clean.
   (b) you can get some pocket money.
   (c) it is cheap.
   (d) it fills the land sometimes.

4. Which word in the text means 'thrown out'?

   _____

5. Which of these statements are true?
   (a) Most household waste is buried.
   (b) Australia has one of the best recycling programs.
   (c) Recycling makes us find new landfill areas.
   (d) Landfill areas are easy to find.

Spelling and Vocabulary

Rewrite the misspelt words.

6. Beet the eggs using the hand mixer.

   _____

7. The bessed jeans I have are the dark blue ones.

   _____

Circle the word that has the nearest meaning to the underlined word.

8. Are you <u>game</u> to tell your parents?
   (a) going   (b) gain
   (c) ready   (d) willing

9. The <u>inside</u> of the house has been repainted.
   (a) interior   (b) middle
   (c) in   (d) outside

Circle the correct word in brackets.

10. Pandas are patterned in black and (wite, white).

11. Who's been eating porridge from my (ditch, dish)?

12. Santa parked his (dear, deer) near the barbeque.

Grammar and Punctuation

13. Underline the **adjectives** in these sentences.

    The fish shop is busy. That man with the straw hat enjoys fresh seafood. See his new car?

14. Punctuate and capitalise this sentence.

    our school song is called always do your best

    _____

    _____

Mathematics

Number and Algebra

1. Follow this addition path.

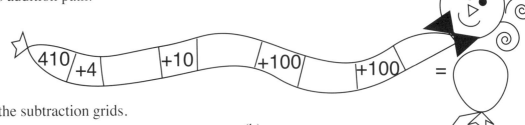

410 | +4 | +10 | +100 | +100 | =

2. Complete the subtraction grids.

(a)

Subtract 4									
9	11	6	4	8	5	10	7	23	82

(b)

Subtract 5									
10	7	15	5	12	6	11	8	94	33

3. Complete the multiplication grids.

(a)

×	2	6	3	8	10	4	7	5	9
3									
6									

(b)

×	5	2	7	3	8	4	9	6	10
9									
1									

4. Complete:

(a)

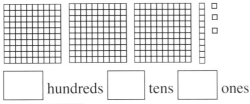

☐ hundreds ☐ tens ☐ ones

= ☐

(b)

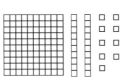

☐ hundreds ☐ tens ☐ ones

= ☐

5. Complete: (a) 500, 501, 502, 503, 504, ☐ , ☐ , ☐ , ☐ , ☐

(b) 900, 800, 700, 600, 500, ☐ , ☐ , ☐ , ☐ , ☐

(c) 310, 320, 330, ☐ , ☐ , ☐ , ☐ , ☐ , ☐

(d) 620, 618, 616, ☐ , ☐ , ☐ , ☐ , ☐

6. (a) Make 3 shares

(b) Make 9 shares.

7. Draw one dollar's worth of 10c coins in this purse.

Measurement and Geometry

8. Look at the clocks below. How many more minutes are there until the next o'clock?

(a) ☐   (b) ☐   (c) ☐   (d) ☐

9. Paul weighs thirty-two kilograms and Peter weighs forty kilograms. How much heavier is Peter than Paul?

☐

10. Complete: (a) 1 m = ☐ cm   (b) 5 m = ☐ cm   (c) 9 m = ☐ cm

11. The children at the cake stall covered the tables with plastic. Which group of tables needed the most plastic?

(a)   (b)   (c)   (d)   ☐

12. Each glass holds half a litre. Colour in the number of glasses that will make three litres.

13. Dip one face of a cube into a bowl of paint and then press it on a piece of paper. What shape have you made?

☐

14. Mai built a toy box with an open top like this: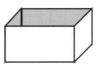

Colour in the pieces of cardboard that she used.

15. On this dot paper, draw a sharp angle. Use your ruler and pencil.

. . . .
. . . .
. . . .
. . . .
. . . .

16. Have we used FLIP, SLIDE or TURN to make the coloured shape?

 ☐

Statistics and Probability

17. How many families live in units?

Double-storey House	▲ ▲ ▲ ▲ ▲
Low-set House	■ ■ ■
Unit	● ● ● ● ● ● ●

☐

My birthday party

Yesterday, Mum gave me a fantastic birthday party. I was allowed to invite ten friends from school and we played outside near the sandpit till dinner-time. For afternoon tea, we had sausage rolls, mini pies, sandwich stacks, jam rolls, cupcakes, custard slices, ice-cream and strawberries and lots of soft drinks.

What I liked best of all though was my delicious birthday cake. It was in the shape of a circular swimming pool and the water was made out of jelly. Mum cut the blue jelly into cubes after it was set and tossed the pieces on top of the cake. I helped decorate the cake by making little swimmers out of broken biscuit, marshmallow and licorice bits. It was clever the way Mum used a red lolly as a beachball.

My cake had eight candles on it. I was nervous when I heard the words, Happy Birthday Nicholas, but managed to still blow out the candles in one almighty breath. I'll remember the funniest incident of the afternoon till my next birthday. Rex (my German Shepherd) stuck his nose into the cream of the cake and ran around all arvo trying to lick it off. Billy's cricket set gift was especially cool!

Reading and Comprehension

1. Write down four foods that Mum prepared for the party.

_____

_____

_____

2. Who was having their birthday?
(a) Rex
(b) Mum
(c) Billy
(d) Nicholas

3. Where did the children play?
(a) in the backyard
(b) in the front yard
(c) near the sandpit
(d) at school

4. *Arvo* is short for
(a) hooray.
(b) horoo.
(c) around.
(d) afternoon.

5. Number these sentences in order (1–4).
(a) The jelly had set.
(b) I helped decorate the cake.
(c) The cake was round.
(d) Mum cut it into cubes.

Spelling and Vocabulary

Rewrite the misspelt words.

6. We plaid near the sandpit.

_____

7. The cake was in the shape of a circul.

_____

Circle the word that has the nearest meaning to the underlined word.

8. My cake was <u>delicious</u>.
(a) tasty
(b) delicate
(c) dull
(d) good

9. They were made out of <u>broken</u> biscuits.
(a) bitter
(b) little
(c) beautiful
(d) crushed

Circle the correct word in brackets.

10. The cake had (ate, eight) candles on it.

11. Mum used a (read, red) lolly as a beachball.

12. I was (aloud, allowed) to have ten guests.

Grammar and Punctuation

13. Underline the **verbs** used in these sentences.

I helped decorate the cake. Mum cut the blue jelly into pieces. I liked the birthday cake very much.

14. Rewrite these sentences and put in the capital letters.

(a) i invited ten friends to my party.

_____

(b) have you seen billy's gift?

_____

(c) susan and frank were invited too.

_____

Number and Algebra

1.

+	56	66	76	86	96	106
8						

2.

−	8	80	800	18	188	88
8						

3.

×	10	20	30	40	50	100
5						

4. Circle the tens digit in 983.

5. 991, ☐ , ☐ , 994, ☐ , ☐ , 997

6.

How many groups of 4 fish are there in 24? ☐

7. How many 20c coins have the same value as $2? ☐

Measurement and Geometry

8. Which season is missing?

Spring, Summer, ☐ , Winter

9. Who is the heaviest and by how much?

Nathaniel 36 kg   Elsa 42 kg   Mary-Lou 39 kg

☐

10. Write these in centimetres.

(a) 1 m 36 cm = ☐ cm

(b) 3 m 35 cm = ☐ cm

11. Shade thirty-five hundredths.

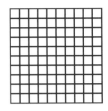

12. Would you use litres to measure a cup of milk? Explain your answer.

☐

13. Name the plane shape that has:
- all sides equal in length
- opposite sides parallel
- no angles equal to 90°.

_____ _____ _____ _____ _____

14. Find an object around you that looks like a rectangular prism. Sketch it.

15. Draw a straight angle and mark it angle X.

16. **Turn** this bottle to the left.

Statistics and Probability

17. What is the total number of coloured cars seen?

☐

Tally	Colour
|||	Blue
ℍℍ	Red
ℍℍ |||	Yellow

David's dictionary

high	97	holiday

high—higher, highest
1.   Rising much above the ground or other object. (adjective)
Mt Kosciuszko is the highest mountain in Australia.

him
1.   The form for *he* when used as an object in a sentence. (pronoun)
They gave him the bottle.

hinge—hinges
1.   A movable joint on which a door, gate, lid hangs and turns. (noun)
Doors have hinges.

hippopotamus—hip-po-pot-a-mus
1.   Large African animal with thick skin living near or in rivers. (noun)

his
1.   Belonging to a man, male or boy. (pronoun)
The cat ate his dinner.

hoarse
1.   Having a harsh, rough voice. (adjective)
She cheered until she was hoarse.

hole—holes
1.   Hollow place in solid body. (noun)
There's a hole in my bucket.
2.   Place where rabbits and foxes live. (noun)

holiday—hol-i-day—holidays
1.   Special days celebrated by stopping work. (noun)
Anzac Day is a holiday in April.
2.   Vacation (noun)
School holidays occur for 12 weeks of the year.

Reading and Comprehension

1.   Which word means that you have a rough voice?
(a) horse   (b) hole
(c) hinge   (d) hoarse

2.   What part of speech is the word underlined here?
My father washed <u>his</u> hair.
(a) verb   (b) noun
(c) adjective   (d) pronoun

3.   Which one is the plural of the word *hinge*?
(a) hinjes   (b) hings
(c) hingies   (d) hinges

4.   What page is David reading? _____

5.   Arrange these words in alphabetical order.
holiday, hinge, hoarse, hippopotamus

_____

Spelling and Vocabulary

Rewrite the misspelt words.

6.   He was probably to busy to think of it.

_____

7.   The tayble was set for six guests.

_____

Circle the word that has the nearest meaning to the underlined word.

8.   It's <u>hard</u> running that fast for five minutes.
(a) easy   (b) strong   (c) helpful   (d) difficult

9.   <u>Hand</u> me the salt please Nicholas.
(a) find   (b) pass
(c) past   (d) fill

Circle the correct word in brackets.

10.   When playing (chest, chess) try and hold on to the Queen.

11.   His foot was caught under the (long, log).

12.   It is half (past, passed) two.

Grammar and Punctuation

13.   Underline the **nouns** in these sentences.

Mary loves collecting stickers. She has pictures of bears, lions and dogs. She puts them in an album.

14.   Punctuate and capitalise this sentence.

i picked up my togs cap towel powder and sunscreen and went to the pool

_____

_____

Number and Algebra

1.

+	112	114	116	118	120	119
9						

2.

–	120	119	118	117	116	121
9						

3.

÷	100	200	300	400	500	550
10						

4. In 8<u>8</u>8 the underlined digit is worth:
(a) 8   (b) 800   (c) 80

5. 460, [   ] , 480, 490, [   ] ,
510, [   ]

6. Share these straws between 2 girls.

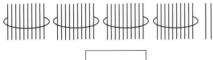

One share is [   ] straws.

7. Complete:
(a) $1.65 = [   ] dollar [   ] cents
(b) $0.80 = [   ] dollars [   ] cents
(c) $1.45 = [   ] cents

Measurement and Geometry

8. Write yesterday's day, date and month.

[   ]

9. How many packets of washing powder do I need to make 20 kg?

 [   ] packets

10. Use the short form to show 1 metre and 15 centimetres. [   ]

11. Is the cover of your Maths book more or less than a square metre? [   ]

12. Name 3 items bought by the litre.

1. [   ]
2. [   ]
3. [   ]

13. Put in the missing letters. My face is:

(a) circu __ __ __

(b) triang __ __ __ __

(c) rectang __ __ __ __

14. Circle which of these solid shapes could have made this sand print.

cube, cone, square pyramid, sphere, cylinder

15. Draw any 4-sided polygon. How many angles does it have?
[   ] [   ]

16. Slide this picture to the right.

Statistics and Probability

17. How many coins were collected altogether? [   ]

20c	50c	$1	$2

The clockface

When you really think about it, a clock has a funny face. It has no eyes, no nose and no mouth. Right in the middle of the clockface is a central point where two arms meet. One hand is short and the other hand long. Both of them move. The short hand moves more slowly than the long hand.

The short hand is the hour hand and the long hand is called the minute hand. The easiest time to tell is when the long hand points straight to twelve. We say it's something o'clock.

When the long hand points to the twelve and the short hand points to the seven, it's seven o'clock. When the long hand points to the twelve and the short hand points to the eleven, it's eleven o'clock.

The minute hand tells you about the minutes, of course! We don't have to read each mark on the circular edge of the clock—just look at the numbers instead. From one number to the next number is five minutes. By now, you should know how to count in fives but just in case you've forgotten, here's a reminder …

… five, ten, fifteen, twenty, twenty-five, thirty, thirty-five, forty, forty-five, fifty, fifty-five, sixty.

Reading and Comprehension

1. The hour hand is
   (a) short.   (b) long.
   (c) central.   (d) numbered.

2. When the long hand points to twelve, and the short hand points to ten, it is
   (a) one o'clock.   (b) ten o'clock.
   (c) 10:10.   (d) 10 to 12.

3. What is the correct spelling of 40?
   (a) fourty   (b) forty
   (c) fourtey   (d) fortieth

4. Complete this pattern.

   60, 55, 50, ____, ____, ____, ____, ____,

   ____, 15, 10, 5

5. Number these morning times in order (1–4).
   (a) eleven o'clock
   (b) one o'clock
   (c) eight o'clock
   (d) five o'clock

Spelling and Vocabulary

Rewrite the misspelt words.

6. Like humans, pandas get two sets of teef.

   _____

7. You can watch the video onlee once.

   _____

Circle the word that has the nearest meaning to the underlined word.

8. The game on Saturday is at Mowley Park.
   (a) match   (b) dance
   (c) test   (d) gain

9. Go to the shop and change this skirt for a bigger one.
   (a) sell   (b) exchange
   (c) hand   (d) purchase

Circle the correct word in brackets.

10. Billy came in third (plase, place).

11. I am (prowd, proud) that Mum is a good cook.

12. Mick is in a lot of (pane, pain).

Grammar and Punctuation

13. Underline the **adjectives** in these sentences.

    The robot with the round nose made a squeaky noise. It moved in a slow way. It had a grey coat on.

14. Punctuate and capitalise this sentence.

    where are the next olympic games going to be held

    _____

    _____

Number and Algebra

1.

+	110	120	210	220	310	390
10						

2.

−	500	400	300	200	100	110
10						

3.

×	1	2	3	4	5	10
12						

4. What is the value of the middle digit in 659?

5. 901, 801, 701, ____, ____, ____, ____

6. Shade in half. How many hundredths are there in this?

7. Can the amount of money in Tom's purse be traded for a $2 coin—yes or no?

Measurement and Geometry

8.

Time	Read as	It means
(a) 2:08		
(b) 7:15		
(c) 4:55		

9. A library book weighs 2 kg. Six of these would weigh a mass of ____ kg.

10. Find out what your height is.

Estimate =

Measure =

11. Find the area of **2** of these shapes.

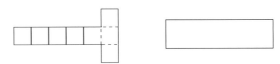

12. A bathtub holds about:
(a) 3 L (b) 10 L (c) 50 L
(d) 800 L (e) 1 L (f) 999 L
(g) half a litre

13. The square below is the shape of a farm. How far is it around the farm?

20 m

14. If I look down on the top of this shape I see a:

15. Colour the angles greater than right-angles in red.

16. Which picture shows a **turn**?

(a)   (b)   (c)

Statistics and Probability

17. How many different kinds of things are shown on this graph?

pens	
pencils	
rubbers	
rulers	

Jack finds the Outback

One Friday night Jack went to stay with Dad for the weekend. Jack knew his father was getting ready to go to the outback again, because of the things he had put in the hall.

There was Dad's swag, which was like a canvas sleeping-bag with a mattress on the bottom. There was a billy. There was an old pencilcase that had once belonged to Jack, which Dad used for storing knives and forks. There was the wire basket in which Dad kept a saucepan and a frying pan. There was a tin of Russian tea, which Dad said was the only tea he could drink without milk and sugar. There was an old enamel mug. And there was a big, strong plastic container for water.

"I'm off again," Jack's father said. "Off to the outback."

"How will you know when you get there?" Jack asked.

Then Jack got the surprise of his life, because his dad said: "Well mate, why don't you come with me and find out for yourself?"

"*Really*?" said Jack. "I don't believe it!"

"Mum and I have talked it over and we think it would be worth it for you to miss school for six weeks to get another sort of education."

"What do you mean?" Jack asked.

"Finding out about other people and other ideas and other places," said Dad. "How about it? If you want to come, we'll get you a swag too."

"Do I *want* to?" cried Jack. "You bet!"

From *Jack finds the Outback* by Judith Womersly

Reading and Comprehension

1. What is the name of the canvas sleeping-bag?
   (a) Billy   (b) mug
   (c) outback   (d) swag

2. The only hot drink Jack's dad liked without milk and sugar was
   (a) black tea.   (b) Russian tea.
   (c) billy tea.   (d) water.

3. For how long was Jack going to miss school?
   (a) a weekend   (b) six days
   (c) six weeks   (d) just a Friday

4. Why was Jack so surprised?

   _____

5. Number these sentences in order (1–4).
   (a) Dad said he could go.
   (b) Dad packed a water container.
   (c) Jack saw what Dad had packed.
   (d) Dad had to get Jack a swag.

Spelling and Vocabulary

Rewrite the misspelt words.

6. I like to lik the spoon after
   making chocolate cake. _____

7. Fat-tailed sheap have lots of fat in their tails.

   _____

Circle the word that has the nearest meaning to the underlined word.

8. She had a <u>small</u> piece of cake.
   (a) big   (b) large   (c) generous   (d) little

9. <u>Stick</u> the sheet on a new page.
   (a) pound   (b) glue   (c) write   (d) repeat

Circle the correct word in brackets.

10. The chair leg was slightly (bend, bent).

11. The (gate, gait) was left open.

12. Jody had the (flew, flu).

Grammar and Punctuation

13. Underline the **verbs** in these sentences.

    Use a sharp pair of scissors. Cut along the dotted line. Remember to throw away the scraps. Fold three times.

14. Punctuate and capitalise this sentence.

    harold ran to the ticket office and then boarded the train

    _____

    _____

Number and Algebra

1.

+	20	120	220	320	420	520
20						

2.

–	20	100	80	60	40	110
20						

3.

÷	11	88	66	22	55	99
11						

4. Circle eight hundred and eighty:
818, 808, 880, 888

5. 860, ⬚, 900, 920, ⬚,
⬚, 980

6. Write the fraction shown.

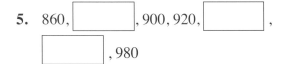

h _ _ _ r _ dths

7. Complete:

Coin used	Amount spent	Change
20c	5c	
50c		40c
10c		0
$1	35c	

Measurement and Geometry

8. Complete these two labels.

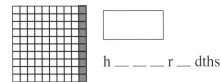

6 : _ _

⬚ past 6

9. Which one is lighter—
a house brick or
4 tablespoons? ⬚

10. Tick the correct answer for 6 longs and 6 shorts.
66 m   66 cm   606 cm

11. Name two things, each with an area less than one square metre.
1. ⬚   2. ⬚

12. Which one is not measured in L?

13. Cross out the shape that doesn't belong.

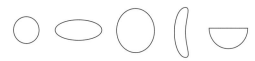

14. How many flat surfaces does this cylinder have?

 ⬚

15. Name this angle.

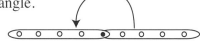

_ _ _ _ _ _ _   _ _ _ _ _

16. Slide this crayon to the right—twice!

_ _ _ _ _ _

Statistics and Probability

17. Draw 6 cars in a row.
If you draw two people between each car, how many people must you draw?

Jobs Vacant

Agents needed to sell books. Must like selling and have own car. Call us on 326 1118 today.

Casual position for anyone who is interested in delivering mail. Good way to keep fit! Only two hours a week. We pay you fifteen dollars an hour. Ring Mark on 334 8877.

Don't go any further! We have just the job for you! Like to wash cars? Do you enjoy sewing? Are you good at typing? Call Mr Smith on 892 0007. We'll find the right job for you today!

Good position for youth 15–17 years as a store packer. We'll train you—no experience necessary. Call us after 9 o'clock tomorrow morning on 381 6176.

Harry's Restaurant requires young boy or girl for assisting the cook. Work till midnight every night. Excellent money. Ring Harry on 384 1624.

Junior helper needed in Southside garage. Phone Jim on 346 9991.

Live-in nanny needed. Must be over 25 years of age. Needed to care for three children aged between 6 and 12. Good pay. Must be able to drive. Phone Mrs Brown on 345 1053.

Reliable person needed to help mow lawns. Must love the outdoors and be able to work every weekend. Call Sally on 326 7784 after 6 pm.

Reading and Comprehension

1. Look at ad number 7. Who would be right for that job?
   (a) Tom—21 years old
   (b) Kim—18 years old
   (c) Mary—26 years old
   (d) Lee—12 years old

2. Look at the second ad. If I worked two hours, I'd get paid
   (a) $15.   (b) $20.
   (c) $35.   (d) $30.

3. William is very good at typing up his stories on the computer. He should call
   (a) 334 8877   (b) 389 1624
   (c) 326 7784   (d) 892 0007

4. What is a nanny? _____

5. Number these sentences from the seventh ad in order (1–4).
   (a) Must be over 25 years of age.
   (b) Live-in nanny needed.
   (c) Must be able to drive.
   (d) Phone Mrs Brown.

Spelling and Vocabulary

Rewrite the misspelt words.

6. You're a site for sore eyes. _____

7. Todae is the first day of spring. _____

Circle the word that has the nearest meaning to the underlined word.

8. I felt <u>alone</u> in the sick-room.
   (a) tired   (b) ill
   (c) isolated   (d) left

9. We heard a loud <u>bang</u> when the glass fell.
   (a) bump   (b) crash
   (c) noise   (d) sound

Circle the correct word in brackets.

10. Grandpa will be home (sune, soon).

11. She (mark, marked) my spelling quickly.

12. You (should, shood) make sure your shoelaces are (tied, tired) well.

Grammar and Punctuation

13. Underline the **verbs** in these sentences.

    The girl was stung by the bee. It hurt her. She cried. I walked her to the office.

14. Punctuate and capitalise this sentence.

    mount cross hospital is right next to dollvale shopping centre

    _____

    _____

Number and Algebra

1.

+	50	100	150	200	250	110
50						

2.

–	50	100	150	200	250	260
50						

3.

×	5	50	100	10	1	15
3						

4. Write the numeral for nine hundred and nineteen.

5. 823, 822, ____, ____, 819, ____, ____,

6. Write the number for:

7. Which silver coin is this size?

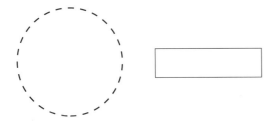

Measurement and Geometry

8. Which season consists of March, April and May?

9. Put in the right word: "I expect six pencil cases to be __ __ __ __ __ __ __ than ten feathers!" said Mr Gramly.

10. The gum tree is 120 cm high. The wattle tree is 5 cm taller. How tall is the wattle tree?

11.
1 m — 1 m

This shows one __ __ __ __ __ __ metre.

12. True or False? A glass holds more than 1 L.

13. Finish this 2D shape pattern.

14. What is the name of the ONLY solid that has no face?

__ __ __ __ __ __ __

15. What is the name given to this type of angle?

16.

This diagram shows that a circle has ____ lines of symmetry.

Statistics and Probability

17. In this picture how many stars can you see?

Colour the blocks to show the stars.

The perfect student

She stood there—just a few centimetres in front of me. She was of average height for a child of nine years. I reckon her weight was about thirty kilograms. I immediately noticed her golden hair. Not one strand was out of place. The part was a straight line and both plaits were exactly the same length. I disliked the red bows at the bottom of the plaits.

You couldn't help but notice the face. It was clean and clear. Her blue eyes sparkled like the sky on a perfect spring day. There certainly were no grubby marks around her mouth and I tried to find a chip in her front teeth, but I couldn't.

This girl had a neat appearance and she must like scrubbing behind the ears! Her school shirt was tucked into the pleated skirt. Both knees were exposed and just below them you could see the socks. They looked brand new because they were sparkling white. Her black school shoes were so well polished that you could see your own reflection.

Yes … I looked up and checked to see that there was no dirt under my nails. I grabbed my new case and hat.

First day of school … here I come …

Reading and Comprehension

1. How old was the girl?
   (a) one
   (b) eight
   (c) nine
   (d) The text doesn't tell you.

2. What was the girl wearing?
   (a) a dress
   (b) her pyjamas
   (c) a school uniform
   (d) jeans and a shirt

3. The last thing she checked was her
   (a) nails.
   (b) shoes.
   (c) hair.
   (d) teeth.

4. The schoolgirl weighed about

   ___ ___ ___ ___ ___ ___ kilograms.

5. Number these sentences in order (1–4).
   (a) She grabbed her case and hat.
   (b) Her shirt was tucked in.
   (c) Her eyes were blue.
   (d) The girl was nine years old.

Spelling and Vocabulary

Rewrite the misspelt words.

6. For lumch I had salmon and cheese sandwiches.

   _____

7. The storem broke out at about midday.

   _____

Circle the word that has the closest meaning to the underlined word.

8. The head of the company was ill.
   (a) director   (b) king
   (c) teacher   (d) principal

9. We don't get a strong flow of water out of the tap.
   (a) drink   (b) test   (c) drowning   (d) gush

Circle the correct word in brackets.

10. I (tryed, tried) to get good marks.

11. (I'd, Ide) like to know how to make pizza.

12. At the coal-mine, the miners let off a (blast, blassed).

Grammar and Punctuation

13. Underline the **nouns** in these sentences.

    Louisa had a project to do. She had to collect rocks. This task had to be done by Thursday.

14. Punctuate and capitalise this sentence.

    i asked whether the treasure chest was for peter or paul

    _____

    _____

    _____

Number and Algebra

1.

+	202	406	518	92	687	199
100						

2.

–	850	750	650	550	450	1000
100						

3.

×	100	200	300	400	500	150
2						

4. How many bundles of 10 can I make out of 591?

5. 499, 500, ____ , ____ , 503, ____ , ____

6. 85 cherries shared by 5.

One share = ____ cherries

7. I only need $1. Cross out any extra coins.

Measurement and Geometry

8. Complete the labels.

(a) 4 : 53   ____ past 4

(b) 7 : 07   ____ past 7

(c) 2 : 30   ____ past 2

9. Does a stepladder weigh more or less than a kilogram? ____

10. 2 metre sticks, 5 longs and 3 shorts

= ____ m ____ cm

11. The classroom whiteboard is more or less than a square metre? ____

12. 5 lots of 10 L = ____ L

13. Cross out the one that doesn't belong.

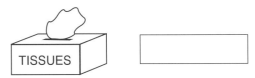

14. How many flat surfaces does this rectangular prism have?

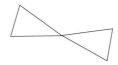 ____

TISSUES

15. What name is given to this type of angle? ____

16. Trace over the point in red, where the **rotation** has occured.

Statistics and Probability

17. How much taller than Anya is the tallest girl? ____

Taylor	97 cm
Christy	82 cm
Anna	1 m 4 cm
Anya	99 cm

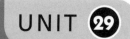

Adam's boat

Adam lived with his parents in a big house in the city. His father went to work every day at his office. When Adam's mother had seen him safely to school, she went to work too. Adam's parents were both very busy people. They never had enough time to fit in all the things they said they wanted to do.

Sometimes Adam's father and mother had to go away. When that happened, Adam went to stay with his grandparents in the country.

Grandma and Grandpa lived with Thomas, their cat, in a small, cosy cottage, close by a wide, slow-moving river.

Adam didn't mind when his parents went away. He loved his grandparents and loved staying with them. They seemed to have all the time in the world. They listened to everything he said, and they told him about all sorts of interesting things. Their cottage was a long drive away from the city, but Adam's parents always took him there. They would stay for a meal, then hug Adam goodbye and remind him to be good.

"He's always good! He's never any trouble!" Grandma would say, putting her arm around Adam. "You can stay away for as long as you can spare him!"

Grandpa, standing close by, would nod in agreement.

From Adam's Boat by Mary Small

Reading and Comprehension

1. Why did Adam have to go to the country?
   (a) His school was there.
   (b) His grandparents lived there.
   (c) Adam's parents had to go away.
   (d) They lived very close to the city.

2. Who was Thomas?
   (a) Grandpa
   (b) the cottage's name
   (c) Adam's dad
   (d) the grandparents' cat

3. Before leaving, Adam's parents would give him a
   (a) present.
   (b) nod.
   (c) warning to be good.
   (d) meal.

4. Who said "He's always good! He's never any trouble!"?

   _____

5. Number these sentences in order (1– 4).
   (a) His grandparents lived in the country.
   (b) They listened to what he said.
   (c) Adam lived in the city.
   (d) His parents were very busy people.

Spelling and Vocabulary

Rewrite the misspelt words.

6. I threw doun my swimming bag. _____

7. The crystal deesh had
   to go on the glass shelf. _____

Circle the word that has the nearest meaning to the underlined word.

8. The flies buzzed around the banana peel.
   (a) skin   (b) cut
   (c) pie   (d) piece

9. The round piece of paper just fit.
   (a) ring
   (b) circular
   (c) circle
   (d) plane

Circle the correct word in brackets.

10. Jane had to (knead, need) the dough.

11. A (told, toad) has rougher skin than a frog.

12. I raced undercover when I saw the dark (grey, gray) clouds.

Grammar and Punctuation

13. Underline the **pronouns** in these sentences.

    She tried on the skirt. It was perfect! Her mother loved the colour. She bought a pink one.

14. Punctuate and capitalise this sentence.

    run nelly run is a great book about a horse

    _____

    _____

Number and Algebra

1.

+	1	10	11	100	101	400
500						

2.

–	900	920	940	960	980	999
500						

3.

÷	20	50	35	40	80	100
5						

4. How many 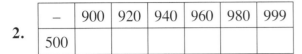 are there in the number 822?

5. Find the missing numbers.

724, [ ] , 728, [ ] , 732, [ ] , [ ]

6. 45 pins shared by 4.

One share = [ ]   Left over = [ ]

7. Count the money.

(50c) (20c) (20c) (20c)

Measurement and Geometry

8. 6:17 — six seventeen

(a) 11:43 — [ ]

(b) 12:57 — [ ]

(c) 5:28 — [ ]

9. What is the total mass of these packages?

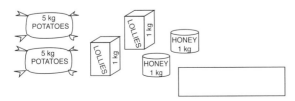

10. The oak tree is 250 cm tall. It is 130 cm taller than me. How tall am I? [ ]

11. In this hundred square, the:

(a) coloured part is [ ] hundredths.

(b) part **not** coloured is [ ] hundredths.

12. What is the total capacity of these containers?

3 L 3 L 1 L 1 L 1 L 1 L   [ ]

13. Draw an irregular hexagon (one with no sides the same).

14. Which two solids each have six faces?
___ ___ ___ ___ and

_____

___ ___ ___ ___ ___.

15. Cross out the triangles that are **not** right angled.

16. Which is a good example of **flip** — (a) or (b)?

(a) 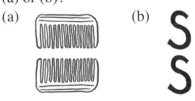   (b) S S

Statistics and Probability

17. Of the three boys who would need the biggest shoe size?

[ ]

Foot length for:	
Max	19 cm
Manny	15 cm
Mel	18 cm

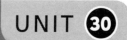

Fabulous fire suit

When Thomas arrived at the fire station, the Fire Chief, a man of considerable size and mild manner, greeted him with a friendly smile. "How can I help you, my boy?" he said.

"It's Mrs McNally," spluttered Thomas. "She's locked herself out and left her keys inside and the kettle's on and . . ."

"Aha!" said the Fire Chief. "This calls for action." And he blew his whistle loudly.

As if by magic, firefighters came sliding down the slippery pole in the middle of the Fire Station. One climbed into the fire engine and started it up. Two more climbed on to the back.

"I'm short-staffed today, Thomas," said the friendly Fire Chief, whose enormous fire suit seemed far too tight for him. "Hop into a suit yourself and come along."

Thomas was a little bit startled by this suggestion, but he needed no second bidding. He took a suit from the wall and put it on. It was the smallest suit there, but even then it was a little large. The trousers were rather long and the coat was rather loose. When he put the belt and boots on, things seemed better. In fact, Thomas felt he had grown a bit, as if his arms and legs were longer and his shoulders wider than before.

"I'm ready!" Thomas said as he jumped up beside the Fire Chief. "Ready to go!"

Whaoo Whaoo Whaooooo screeched the siren as the fire engine raced down the street to the block of flats.

From *Thomas Torrington and the Fabulous Fire Suit* by Gordon Winch

Reading and Comprehension

1. Who was in trouble?
   (a) Mrs McNally   (b) Thomas
   (c) a neighbour   (d) Thomas's grandad

2. How many firefighters were in the fire engine?
   (a) 3   (b) 5   (c) 4   (d) 2

3. The fire suit Thomas wore was
   (a) too tight.   (b) too big.
   (c) small.   (d) just a bit large.

4. Why did Mrs McNally need help?

   _____

5. Number these sentences in order (1–4).
   (a) The Fire Chief blew his whistle.
   (b) The siren screeched.
   (c) Thomas took the suit and put it on.
   (d) Thomas arrived at the fire station.

Spelling and Vocabulary

Rewrite the misspelt words.

6. I tried to drawer a picture of my face.

   _____

7. On Break-Up Day we had to danse Rock'n' Roll.

   _____

Circle the word that has the nearest meaning to the underlined word.

8. Can I <u>help</u> you with anything, sir?
   (a) make   (b) held   (c) assist   (d) spoil

9. The bus was so crowded I was <u>pushed</u> a bit.
   (a) shoved   (b) pleased   (c) sweating   (d) praised

Circle the correct word in brackets.

10. I misjudged the (steep, step).

11. Simon read a great (storey, story).

12. One day I hope to (meet, meat) my (night, knight) in shining armour.

Grammar and Punctuation

13. Underline the **pronouns** in these sentences.

    They went by themselves to our place. We had a picnic. Jerry brought his tapes along.

14. Punctuate and capitalise this sentence.

    do you know where you put my black boots

    _____

    _____

Number and Algebra

1. Follow this addition path.

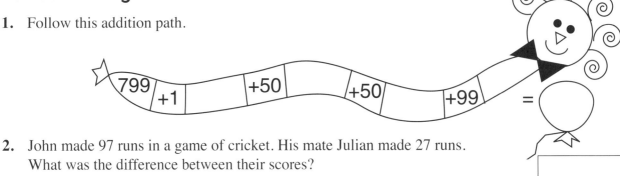

799 +1 +50 +50 +99 =

2. John made 97 runs in a game of cricket. His mate Julian made 27 runs. What was the difference between their scores?

3. How many children could be given 4 cherries each?

(a)   (b)   (c)   (d)

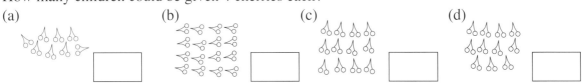

4. Write the number made up of:

(a) 46 tens and 3 ones

(b) 98 tens and 2 ones

(c) 7 hundreds and 56 ones

(d) 50 tens

5. Fill in the missing numbers on these railway lines.

(a)

718   721   724

(b)

582   592

6.

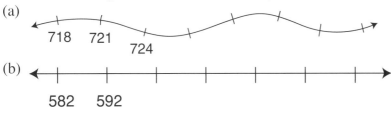

(a) How many squares are there?

(b) What part of the group is coloured?

(c) What part of the group is not coloured?

(d) What part of the group has dots?

7. How many more 20c coins are needed to make $2?

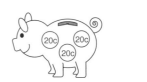

Measurement and Geometry

8. On each clock below, draw the hands to show the time given.

(a) 7 : 10   (b) 6 : 37

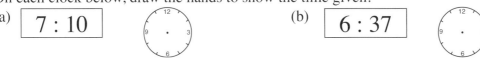

9. How many packets of washing powder do I need to make 60 kg?

10. Circle the objects that are more than 1 metre, and put a tick next to those that are less than 1 metre.

- length of your arm
- length of a bed
- a tall gum tree
- your ruler
- across your room
- a beach umbrella
- length of a path
- length of a street
- length of a truck
- height of a cat

11. How many times is the rectangle used to cover this area?

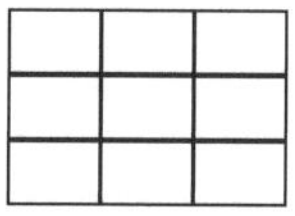

12. Jason collected many containers of different sizes. He used a one-litre container to check the capacity of each. Colour the containers that might hold:

(a) about 1 litre, green   (b) less than 1 litre, blue   (c) more than 1 litre, yellow

Shape	△	□	⬠	⬡	⯃
Name of shape					
Number of sides					
Number of axes of symmetry					

13.

14. Name this solid shape.

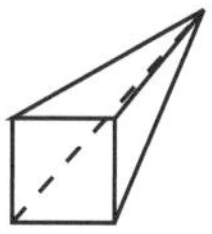

15. Which angle is the sharpest?   X   Y   Z

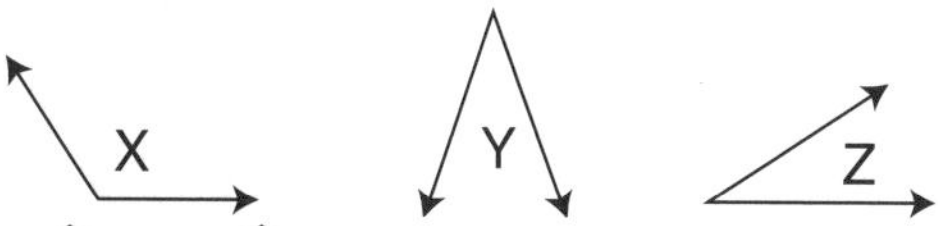

16. Draw in the lines of symmetry.

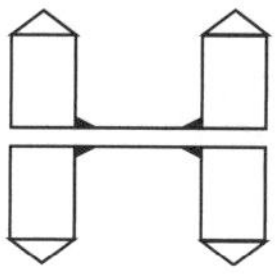

Statistics and Probability

17. How many children were born in Melbourne and Sydney?

Brisbane

Perth

Sydney

Melbourne

Tennis

Tennis is a fun sport played by two or four people. When the game is played by two people it is known as Singles and when the game is played by four people it is called Doubles. Tennis can be played indoors or outdoors, and is often played on a court of grass. Today, a lot of important matches are still played outdoors.

A tennis match is made up of games and sets. The first player to win six games (as long as the opponent has not won more than four) is said to have won the first set. White lines on the court show if the ball is in or out.

Tennis racquets are usually made out of wood, steel or aluminium. Modern racquets have graphite in them. Graphite is a type of lead which has a nice shine and feels slippery. Lead pencils that you write with have graphite in them. Racquets have an oval head. This oval-shaped head is strung with strong threads. Nylon is often used here. The player needs to get a good grip on the handle so the handle is covered with leather or rubber.

For the player's own safety, it is best to wear shoes with non-skid rubber soles. Traditionally, tennis players wore white—from head to toe!

Reading and Comprehension

1. How many players are there in a Doubles game?
   (a) one
   (b) two
   (c) four
   (d) eight

2. Who is the *opponent*?
   (a) player
   (b) runner
   (c) enemy
   (d) umpire

3. *Non-skid* means
   (a) 'non-white'.
   (b) 'not new'.
   (c) 'not safe'.
   (d) 'not slippery'.

4. Why do you think it is important for a racquet to have a good grip?

   _____

   _____

   _____

   _____

5. Number these sentences in order (1– 4).
   (a) It can be played indoors or outdoors.
   (b) Years ago, players wore white.
   (c) Tennis is a fun sport.
   (d) Lines are painted on a tennis court.

Spelling and Vocabulary

Rewrite the misspelt words.

6. The handel can be made out of leather.

   _____

   _____

7. Tenis can be played on grass.

   _____

   _____

Circle the word that has the nearest meaning to the underlined word.

8. Tennis can be played <u>indoors</u>.
   (a) inside
   (b) interestingly
   (c) in
   (d) instantly

9. The head is strung with <u>strong</u> threads.
   (a) weak
   (b) nylon
   (c) safe
   (d) powerful

Circle the correct word in brackets.

10. It is best to (where, wear) good shoes.

11. Racquets can be made out of (steal, steel).

12. The (souls, soles) should be made out of rubber.

Grammar and Punctuation

13. Underline the **nouns** in these sentences.

    Tennis is a ball sport. It can be played by two people. Every player needs a racquet. The handle can be made out of leather.

14. Punctuate and capitalise this sentence.

    tennis racquets are made out of wood steel graphite or aluminium

    _____

    _____

    _____

    _____

© 1998 Harval Pty Ltd and Pascal Press
Reprinted 1998, 1999, 2000, 2001 (twice), 2002, 2003, 2004, 2005, 2007, 2008 (twice), 2010, 2011 (twice)

Updated in 2013 for the Australian Curriculum

Reprinted 2014, 2015, 2016, 2017, 2018, 2019, 2020 (twice), 2021

ISBN 978 1 86441 274 1

Pascal Press
PO Box 250
Glebe NSW 2037
(02) 8585 4044
www.pascalpress.com.au

Publisher: Vivienne Joannou
Project editor: Mark Dixon
Australian Curriculum updates edited by Rosemary Peers and answers checked by Peter Little
Typeset by Precision Typesetting (Barbara Nilsson) and lj Design (Julianne Billington)
Cover by DiZign Pty Ltd
Printed by Vivar Printing/Green Giant Press

Acknowledgements
The following sources for material are kindly acknowledged:
Quiet Pony for Sale by Mary Small
Pandas by Christine Deacon
My Diary by Jenny Jarman-Walker
Charlie's Damper by RL Muddyman
Pet's Day by Celeste Snowdon
When Melissa Ann Came to Dinner by Dianne Bates
Big April Fools! by Edel Wignell
Kzot, the Amazing Robot by Jan Weeks
Simpson and Duffy by Mary Small
Stevie Comes to Stay by Gordon Winch
Kylie the Kangaroo by Gordon Winch
Jack finds the Outback by Judith Womersley
Adam's Boat by Mary Small
Thomas Torrington and the Fabulous Fire Suit by Gordon Winch.